Introduction to Professional Gardening and Landscaping

Claude P. Major, Ph.D.

DARNLEY
PUBLICATIONS
INC.

Legal deposit – Bibliothèque et Archives nationales du Québec, 2010
Legal deposit – Library and Archives Canada, 2010

ISBN 978-2-923623-13-9

Printed in Canada

Catalog Number: TBAC1-1

Author
Claude P. Major, Ph.D.

Editor-in-Chief
Michael Boulay

Project Manager
Francine Hébert, M.Ed.

Copy Editors
Joanne Labre
John Alarie
Matthew Testa

Graphic Designers
Natacha Lavigne
Michael Gonzalez

** Selected images were taken by Natacha Lavigne*

Table of Contents

Introduction

There is an old expression about not being able to see the forest for the trees. Considering that trees are literally a part of gardening and landscaping, the expression applies here both literally and figuratively. What it means is that it is hard to start plunging into technical details and how-to procedures without first having a sense of where you are going, and why the information is important.

As you will shortly discover, the gardening and landscaping "industry" is not a single occupation, or a pair of occupations, but rather a very broad and diversified field of business and aesthetic opportunities. Many readers already have an interest in a particular area when they begin to explore this subject. However, when they discover how many other areas are out there, their interests sometimes change. Careers develop over time. People start out in one place, and then their careers progress naturally as opportunities and experiences present themselves.

Of course, not everyone who reads a text about professional gardening and landscaping has career aspirations. Some readers are simply very serious hobbyists who are interested in gaining a professional level of knowledge, without necessarily wishing to use it to earn a paycheck. That is fine. The vast majority of this book contains general information about gardening and landscaping that will interest both

hobbyists and aspiring professionals alike. Although we will frequently refer to professional gardeners and landscapers throughout this text, please be aware that serious gardening enthusiasts are always implicitly included in our discussion.

Chapter 1 of this text presents a listing and brief explanation of forty ways in which people can and do earn a living in the field of landscaping and gardening. We hope that this extensive list will get your attention and provide you with some fresh career ideas to add to the ones you already have.

The central portion of this book is an orientation to the basic tasks, activities, and materials of the trade. You will need to understand these basics before you get into more-detailed subject matter. Chapter 2 discusses plants themselves, how to identify them, and the terminology associated with them. Obviously this is core information for anyone who plans to spend a career working with plants.

Next, in chapter 3, we review the basic tasks of garden maintenance. This is not a detailed how-to section, but a broad orientation to exactly what it is that professional gardeners and landscapers do. You may find there are more activities than you first realized. From there we introduce the nonplant aspects of a garden or landscape, including pools, walkways, fences, terraces, and the like. Chapter 4 shows you how the pieces fit together, in its discussion of selecting and using plants in a typical landscape design.

An important element to becoming a gardening pro is understanding the basic mistakes that people tend to make often and repeatedly, and knowing what can be done to avoid or at least mitigate them. Toward that important end, chapter 5 summarizes the ten most common mistakes that landscapers and gardeners, both amateur and professional, tend to make. Gardeners will of course face a variety of challenges, but these ten are some of the most critical. Familiarizing yourself now with these concerns will get you off to a good start.

Finally, since part of the aim of this text is to motivate you and introduce you to the industry, we conclude with a section of breathtaking photos of some of the world's greatest and most famous gardens. Photos of these gorgeous facilities will expose you to an array of stunning possibilities in gardening and landscaping, and they may even inspire you to add new and captivating elements to your own work.

Gardening can be a lot of hard work. But it can also be great, great fun! And if you can have fun and earn a living at the same time, then life is, well, *almost* like a bed of roses.

40 Ways to Make Money in Landscaping and Gardening

All of the business models described in this chapter can and do provide full-time income to some gardening entrepreneurs out there. However, many of them also serve as opportunities for part-time incomes or home-based business ventures that, like plants themselves, may start small and eventually grow larger. It is also possible to combine some of these opportunities in order to diversify, acquire new clients for a pre-existing business, or add new lines of products or services to another type of landscaping or gardening business.

Some of these businesses can be started with only the training one receives in a typical landscaping and gardening course. Others require some additional skills or expertise. Some of these activities may also appeal to enthusiastic, dedicated hobbyists whose interest lies more in gardening for pleasure than for business.

Not every gardener pursues gardening as a career strategy. There are many who are drawn to it as a hobby, and perhaps over time some will develop an interest in making a little money at it. Even if you do not expect to make gardening your career, the activities and business opportunities described in this chapter may still inspire you with new ideas for your own personal projects and aspirations, whatever your motivations.

General Landscaping Business

This is the largest single opportunity both for employment and entrepreneurship within the industry. Its fundamental activities form the basis of most traditional books on landscaping, including this one. However, even this one business format is really a variety of slightly different businesses grouped under the same umbrella.

Most general landscaping contractors will take on almost any work related to gardening and landscaping that they can get, including both landscape installation and grounds maintenance. However, depending on the size of the operation, where it is located, and the expertise and ambitions of the owners, the proportions of time and income derived from specific landscaping activities can vary greatly. Some businesses get most of their work in suburban neighborhoods, mowing lawns, raking leaves, assisting the elderly or disabled with maintaining the gardens and shrubbery on their properties, and looking after properties for people away on vacation. Other businesses are much more active in landscape design and in the creation of new gardens and landscapes of varying degrees of expense and sophistication.

Some landscapers get significant work from construction contractors. For example, when a construction contractor puts in a new subdivision, the landscaping business may be hired to lay down sod, plant trees, and install beds of shrubbery around the front of the home. In a subdivision where many nearly identical homes are being created quickly, this can become a little monotonous, with the same types of landscaping performed over and over on each adjacent property. However, such a contract can be lucrative and provide steady work for the firm.

In more upscale neighborhoods, almost every property owner will hire a landscaping service, and the range of duties performed may be more extensive. The lawn will still need to be mowed, but there may also be more-elaborate flower gardens and beds of shrubbery to maintain. Also, some clients will hire a landscaper to plan and produce more-sophisticated garden structures such as pools, gazebos, rock gardens, or even greenhouses or arboretums. Depending on the nature of the work and the size and expertise of the staff, the landscaping company may subcontract some of the project to stonemasons or companies that pour concrete and lay pavement. However, ideally the landscaping business serves as the general contractor on the project, designing the project and supervising the work done by its own staff and by the subcontractors.

Gardening Service

A gardening service is like a landscaping business, but with a particular focus on the creation and maintenance of gardens. This business markets and sells the services of highly knowledgeable professional gardeners.

They may install and maintain large flowerbeds and beds of mixed flowers and shrubs, either for individual clients or sometimes for businesses and public parks. Parks that aren't large enough to hire a full-time gardener may contract for such services.

Lawn Mowing Service

This is a landscaping business that goes after one type of business: grass cutting. In most parts of the country it is a seasonal business, and often it provides summer jobs for students. With enough steady contracts it can earn impressive revenues over the growing season. The appeal of this business model is its simplicity. It can be as basic as a truck, a couple of employees, and a couple of lawnmowers. However, some of these businesses are more sophisticated, with several crews and vehicles on the go at the same time.

Commercial Plant Service (Interior Landscaping)

A commercial plant service is a specialized landscaping business that may be particularly or even exclusively active in indoor urban environments. The service designs, provides, installs, and maintains plants in beds and pots in malls, business properties, offices, and some private residences. Often this will involve caring for perennial foliage plants and small trees, as opposed to flowers. The plants will need regular watering, pruning, and cleaning. A contract may call for large potted plants to be rotated periodically. Sometimes plant services will work with window dressers in stores to provide short-term rentals of plants that will be part of a decorating scheme. They may also provide plants to businesses or events as diverse as public festivals or the sets of film productions. Essentially, clients of this service want to have plants but they do not necessarily want to own them permanently or be responsible for their care.

Flower and Plant Store

This is the main retail arm of the industry. It involves a shop, often in a shopping mall, that sells live plants, dried floral arrangements, cut flowers, and indoor plant care accessories to consumers. Depending on the location and style of the business, a lot of the work may involve cut flowers and the production of floral arrangements for holidays and special events. Although this segment of the industry is often quite competitive, these stores can be very profitable.

Garden Center (Nursery)

A garden center is somewhat different from a retail flower and plant store in that it caters to home gardeners and usually specializes in outdoor plants. It offers shrubs, small trees, transplants, seeds, and accessories. In some regions, garden centers are able to operate year-round. In other places they are seasonal businesses.

A recent trend is the temporary garden center that may be set up by a supermarket, hardware store, or shopping mall. It opens in spring, often setting up in a portion of a parking lot using canvas tents to shelter some of its merchandise from the elements. By the end of June or early July, when most homeowners have planted everything they intend to plant that season, these centers shut down and pack up. Those centers that produce their own live merchandise may have a greenhouse or other facility where they raise the product in the off-season, so that they may have a suitable quantity of small shrubs and transplants available at the peak planting season.

Produce Grower

Here is an occupation that all but vanished, but is now making a strong comeback. The rebound is in part thanks to public awareness about the threat of global warming and the high energy costs associated with shipping produce from distant corners of the planet. Many consumers "buy local" as much as possible, and even large supermarket chains are making a renewed effort to buy from local growers when they can.

You don't need a large farm to get in on this. Five to ten acres of land will often suffice to operate at least a modest seasonal-vegetable business. One advantage of staying small is the opportunity to sell directly to the public rather accept the wholesale prices offered by supermarkets and other resellers. Roadside vegetable stands, portable stands set up in parking lots, selling at farmers' markets and flea markets, and even selling from a truck on the side of the road are all making a comeback. This is not something apt to provide a year-round income in most North American climates, but it can be coupled with other gardening or farming ventures to help boost the family income. The key to success is providing fresh produce at competitive prices and building a base of loyal customers. Some sellers also expand their product line to include items such as fresh-baked pies and breads, cider, and other prepared products that appeal to the vegetable purchaser.

Organic Produce Farming

Organically grown produce is increasingly popular, and it can be profitable enough that smaller growers can support themselves in this field. Once again, you don't necessarily need to have hundreds of acres of land and heavy-duty farm machinery. The challenge, however, is to learn all of the organically acceptable options for soil enrichment and pest control. This time the market is not usually selling directly to the public from a roadside stand, but rather selling through specialty markets that carry organic produce for their health-conscious clientele.

Grower of Herbs and Spices

Here's another type of specialty farming that doesn't necessarily require huge tracts of land. Many specialty shops and produce sellers purchase herbs and spices, whether fresh or dried, from small local vendors, and offer them as alternatives to the mass-produced dried spice bottles sold by supermarkets. Another potential market is fine dining restaurants, where the chefs may appreciate the freshness and unique quality of what you can offer them.

Specialty Grower

A specialty grower sells horticultural products other than fruits and vegetables. There are many different businesses that belong to this category. Some of them are just side projects of plant enthusiasts, and bring in only enough income to support the owner's own gardening hobby. Others are large and successful businesses with hundreds of thousands of dollars in sales to garden centers, and often directly to consumers via direct mail and the Internet. These companies grow plants and flowers that require some special expertise and that go beyond the capabilities of the typical garden center supplier. For example, they may produce special hybrids of roses, irises, orchids, bonsai trees, and other popular flowering plants and shrubs. Some specialty growers go so far as to crossbreed and engineer their own unique strains. They cater to those who enter or attend gardening competitions, and they may participate in such events themselves. They may also make the rounds of home-gardening expositions and trade shows, promoting their special lines of bulbs and live plants for sale.

Seed Grower and Seller

The aim here is to produce and sell the seeds that people tend to buy for planting their own vegetable and flower gardens. There are two basic business models. One is really a variation on the retail garden center, but with increased emphasis on stocking large quantities and varieties of seeds in addition to transplants or other live plants for sale. The other model is the wholesale and mail-order seed company. Individual gardeners and garden centers place orders by mail or over the Internet in advance of the new growing seasons, and the company ships the seeds by mail or courier in time for planting.

Seed growers may also farm much of the crop that they will use as the sources of their seeds. However, since it is typically necessary to offer such a wide range of seeds, most sellers enter into arrangements with other farmers or growers to produce some of the crop they will harvest and render as seeds.

Wholesaler or Retail Grower of Potted Plants

Today you can find potted plants for sale in almost every large grocery and department store, and there is a whole segment of the industry that produces and distributes them. Many are grown in greenhouses. However, as you will soon learn, it is possible for anyone to construct a simple greenhouse on his or her property. Therefore, raising and selling potted plants need not be a large commercial venture with a huge capital investment.

Online Sales of Gardening Supplies

Online shopping has opened new business opportunities for entrepreneurs in every industry, including gardening. Rather than having to print costly product catalogs and acquire mailing lists of people to send them to, today a seller can advertise and display a product line on a website, which can also take and process orders. Virtually anything that is sold in gardening shops, flower shops, and hardware stores can be offered online, and without the expense of having to maintain a store.

Manufacturing and Distributing Compost and Mulch

Plants are only some of the "consumables" needed by this industry and its patrons. Another important product line involves the production and distribution of topsoil, potting soil, compost, organic fertilizers, manure, and mulch. These producers may sell to garden centers, department stores, and sometimes directly to the public. This is

often essentially a farming operation, but rather than or in addition to crops, the farm generates peat, composed organic waste, enriched soil, bark chips, and other related products.

Worm Rancher

You may be surprised to discover how many people are making a nice living at worm ranching. (Check out the Internet, which is the main way these companies advertise and sell their product.) There are two basic types of what most people would think of simply as earthworms. The type that is common in most lawns and gardens feeds by ingesting soil and filtering microorganisms from it. In doing so they help break down some organic materials in the soil, making the nutrients more readily available to plants. The second type is the composting worm that doesn't live in soil, but rather in decomposing organic waste. It resembles the earthworm but its environment is quite different. This second type of worm is especially useful in creating compost, so these worms are in demand for persons who wish to make compost for their own gardens. They also appeal to environmentally conscious homeowners who wish to process some of their own organic waste so less of it is sent to landfills.

Another advantage of composting-type worms is that they reproduce readily and fairly quickly in captivity. This allows them to be raised and sold commercially, rather than collected from the environment. Earthworms that feed in soil, such as night crawlers, are more difficult to raise in large quantities in a farming operation. Both types of worms make excellent fishing bait, which can be quite profitable.

Worm farming can complement other opportunities and business models in gardening, farming, and livestock raising. Almost any farming or growing operation will generate enough organic waste that can be put to good use by raising worms as a sideline.

Sod Grower

Sod (rolled strips of live grass that can be unrolled to create an instant lawn) has become a big part of the landscaping industry. Almost no one these days installs a new lawn from seed. It takes some special expertise to be able to grow and harvest sod, but there is a strong market for those who do it well.

Golf Grass Grower

Speaking of sod, here's a specialty field that is relatively small, but often lucrative for those who do well in it. You may not realize that the grass grown and installed on golf course greens is a very special variety that requires considerable expertise to produce. For many of the better golf country clubs, the greens are the most expensive part of the development costs after the clubhouse itself. This grass is often produced in special growing operations and then transported and installed in the form of sod. What is special about the grass is its density and its ability to survive extremely close mowing.

Peat Harvester

Peat moss is a very important gardening and landscaping material. It grows under special conditions, and in some locations it grows extensively in wild areas that are not suitable for any other form of agriculture. If you own the right land, this can be an attractive option for you.

Christmas Tree Farmer

Here's another specialty operation you may not think of immediately. Growers need special knowledge of the handful of evergreen species grown as Christmas trees. They also need to understand and be able to access the marketing and distribution channels.

There are two types of tree growers, large and small. Large growers annually produce a sizeable harvest that is distributed through wholesalers or networks of sellers. Small growers often produce their own trees and sell them directly to the public via one of two methods, or a combination of both. The first method is to invite the public onto the farm to select and cut their own trees. The second is to harvest the trees and sell them through seasonal stands set up in urban and suburban centers, sometimes in parking lots or on vacant land adjacent to popular shopping areas.

The demand remains strong for this product, especially as consumers want more "natural" holidays without the environmental consequences of artificial trees that eventually wear out and end up in landfills. Natural

Christmas trees, besides being fragrant and beautiful, are biodegradable. In fact, a secondary business activity exists to grind up discarded trees and turn them into mulch or compost.

Topiary Designer

If you feel there is a bit of an artist or sculptor in you, but you also love working with plants, this may be the specialty field for you. Topiary is the art of training and pruning small trees and shrubs into special decorative shapes. The shapes may resemble objects or animals, or they may simply create some abstract or geometric design. This requires some special expertise on top of knowledge of gardening and landscaping. Success of the topiary installations depends on selecting the right species, planting in the proper conditions and density, pruning and adjusting the shrubs as they grow, and then regularly pruning the branches and leaves to create and maintain the finished form. Demand for topiary designers is usually greater in more affluent neighborhoods.

Producing and Distributing Homemade Preserves and Pickles

Some people enjoy growing their own produce and then adding value to it with some simple processing. With the right recipes and the right business skills, this can be a rewarding and profitable cottage industry. Products may be sold online or at specialty food stores, craft fairs, or flea markets.

Maple Syrup or Birch Syrup Producer

Here's another specialized form of farming that has room for both large and small players. Obviously you need to own a stand of maple (or sometimes birch) trees in a climate that is suitable for maple sugar production. Fortunately, the equipment you need to collect and process the syrup can be simple and inexpensive. Some take it a step further and process the syrup into maple sugar candies or other treats.

Producer of Fruit and Vegetable Juices

There are both giant corporations and small, specialty operations that make and sell juice. Smaller players need to offer some reason why their juices, which will probably be more expensive than the mass-produced supermarket versions, are worth buying. This may involve special blends, added nutritional value, or certified organic produce and processing. It is important, however, that persons who attempt to enter this field learn all of the health and safety issues and regulations related to food processing.

Dried Flower Production and Arrangement

Flower shops and many other retailers sell dried flowers, but few of them cultivate the product themselves. Rather, they obtain it from suppliers who actually grow, cut, and dry the flowers, and in some cases assemble the arrangements. One interesting thing about this specialty is you can harvest some wildflowers and plants to supplement those you grow or purchase from other growers. This business can start out small and simple yet still be a profitable venture.

Rented Garden Plots and Agricultural Leasing

Here's an option that doesn't require you to do anything at all other than own land. In rural areas close to a city there is a growing market for renting out small plots to city folks who want a taste of the gardening experience but don't have the opportunity to do it where they live.

As an alternative to renting small plots to numerous clients, some landowners lease vast areas of land for large-scale farming operations. As global demand for food rises, it is becoming necessary to find new land that can be devoted to agriculture.

Urban Rooftop Horticulture

Here's another specialty industry that didn't exist twenty years ago but is rapidly increasing in interest as people become more concerned about the environment. It involves turning the roofs of buildings into gardens. Sometimes this is done for aesthetic purposes, but increasingly people are learning about the benefits of urban gardens for building insulation and dealing with air pollution.

People who enter this profession need to know all the usual array of information about gardening. However, they must also work closely with architects and engineers to ensure that structures can withstand the weight of a rooftop garden and accommodate its water and drainage needs.

Garden Theme Park

Another option is setting up a garden in or close to an urban area, and then converting it into an agricultural theme park. Under organized supervision, guests may tour the grounds, watch gardeners in action, learn about farming and gardening methods, and sometimes gain a bit of hands-on experience. Besides being a refreshing oasis of greenery, the theme park can also serve as an educational center, offering lectures and workshops on gardening topics.

Gardening Courses and Workshops

It is not necessary to open a garden theme park in order to offer courses and workshops. All you need is the gardening know-how, the people skills, and a place to meet. This may be on your property, or it can also take place at a public library, local school, or community center.

U-Pick Fruit and Vegetable Farm

Many farms located near population centers open themselves up at harvest time and let consumers drive up, walk through the fields or orchards, and pick their own produce. The customers usually save some money over supermarket prices, but that isn't the main attraction. People come for the experience, which can be fun for the entire family. These farms often engage in more conventional agricultural activities, and also offer other recreational opportunities and related products to visitors.

Harvest Festival

This business encourages nearby residents and tourists to flock to an area for a special harvest festival, which may last anywhere from a weekend to a month or longer. The festival may include musical entertainment, exhibitions, rides and other fun activities, and food service. Obviously this is not a year-round enterprise, but it can be a very lucrative addition to some other gardening venture.

Hydroponics

Hydroponics involves the growing of plants in water rather than soil. It is an indoor gardening method that has many enthusiasts. This is a specialized area of gardening, and those who acquire expertise in its equipment and methods can sell supplies and services to hydroponic growers.

Tree Cutting and Pruning

Arborists, or "tree surgeons," take down dead trees and repair damaged ones. Some special equipment is needed to perform this work. Arborists also need the same general knowledge of the cultivation and propagation of trees and shrubs as others in the gardening and landscaping professions.

Firewood Sales

Anyone who owns a woodlot that features mature hardwood trees has an opportunity to make some extra income cutting and selling firewood. Again, this is a niche market that is on the

upswing as fuel prices rise and more and more people look to less-expensive, renewable solutions for home heating. The business is sustainable as long as only old and dying trees or deadwood are harvested, and replanting is done to ensure renewed growth.

Tree Planting

Tree planting is a job that appeals to more and more young people these days, because it is both ecologically beneficial and a way of working in the great outdoors. Forestry companies hire tree planters to help renew areas that have been logged. In addition, many groups plant trees to slow global warming and to repay the carbon debt that is incurred through activities such as air travel. Trees take carbon dioxide out of the air, so they are the best natural defense against greenhouse gases.

Horticultural Pest Control

This is the agricultural version of the exterminator, a person who consults with farmers or property owners about pest control and offers both chemical and organic solutions.

Paving and Masonry

Plants are by no means the only type of supplies and services involved in gardening and landscaping. Opportunities exist to manufacture, sell, install, and service the other components of landscape and garden design. Garden installation also often involves the creation of paved or stone walkways, walls, fountains, pools, and other decorative or functional structures.

Stonework is in particularly high demand. Most landscapers lack the expertise to do complex stonework, so they contract out for this service when it becomes an element in the landscape design. Sometimes the contract is issued by the home builder.

Custom Pottery and Ceramics

Ceramic decorations and pots are also commonly used in gardening and landscaping. The production of ceramics is a specialized occupation, but one that attracts much of its business from gardeners, who often request customized products.

Soil and Water Testing and Environmental Consulting

This is another specialty that goes beyond the expertise of the landscaper, but that often works closely with a landscaping firm on an overall design. Aesthetic appeal is not the only issue to consider when designing a landscape. There are topographical and geological issues that are particular to a location and that affect the functional aspects of the landscaping and what is needed or what will work.

Gardening Writer or Photographer

If you have skills as either a writer or a photographer, or both, there is high demand for these services from horticultural magazines, publishers, websites, and catalog businesses.

Mail-Order Sales of Gardening Books

There are several publishers that specialize in gardening. Selling gardening books online is a convenient way to reach customers around the world. You can resell books produced by commercial publishing houses, or become a book publisher yourself, depending on your own talents, resources, and inclinations.

Understanding and Identifying Plants

Plants literally cover the earth's surface. A landscape without any plants seems unnatural or forbidding. Plants are found on all types of land, from arctic tundra to tropical rainforest. They also are found in both fresh and salt water.

Because of the tremendous differences in ecological conditions, each region has special plant life that thrives there, from graceful sea fans in the ocean to water-conserving cacti in the desert. Each plant tells us something about the conditions of its habitat.

Plants are classified in various ways. This can be confusing since more than one term is used to describe the same plant, but the terms are also very helpful to the landscape designer and gardener. Understanding these terms will allow you to quickly determine the basic growing habits of plants you may use in a project.

Plant Lifespans

Plants may be classified by their lifespans. Annual plants normally complete their entire life cycle during one growing season. Marigolds and spinach are examples of annuals. Flowering annuals, like marigolds and petunias, are used to add color to landscapes throughout the growing season, since they usually bloom continuously.

Biennials are plants that complete their entire life cycle in two growing seasons. During the first growing season, a biennial is usually low growing and leafy. After the cold temperatures in the winter, the plant "bolts," or sends up, a bloom stalk that flowers and goes to seed in the second growing season. Cabbage, celery, and evening primrose are biennials.

Perennials are plants that grow year after year and often take many years to mature. There are perennial flowers, such as lilies and daisies. Although flowering perennials come back every year, they usually bloom for shorter periods of time than flowering annuals. Asparagus and rhubarb are perennial vegetables. The above-ground plant dies in the winter in temperate regions, but the roots stay alive and grow again in the spring.

Trees and shrubs are also perennial plants. Trees and shrubs differ from other plants previously discussed because they have woody stems that survive year after year.

The lifespan of some plants depends on the region where they grow. For example, subtropical perennials such as tomato, eggplant, and coleus, are grown as annuals in temperate climates since they cannot survive the cold winters. Carrots, cabbage, and beets are biennials that are used as annuals, since they are harvested after the first season.

Growth Habits of Plants

Plants can also be classified according to their growth habits. Herbaceous plants have fleshy stems that usually die down to soil level in the winter. Annuals and biennials are herbaceous plants. Woody plants are shrubs, trees, some vines, and some perennial plants. Their stems, of course, are made of wood.

Trees are characterized by a single central axis or trunk. Shrubs have several stems that are more or less upright. Trees are usually larger than shrubs.

Another classification method is based on whether the plants keep their leaves in the winter. Deciduous plants lose their leaves in the winter. Evergreens keep their leaves all year long. There are deciduous shrubs, such as some dogwoods. Rhododendron is an evergreen shrub. Evergreen trees include spruces, pines, and firs. Birches and maples are examples of deciduous trees.

Horticultural Terms

Horticulture is the art and science of cultivating the many plants that are used in landscaping and gardening. Horticulturalists divide plants into two basic categories: *ornamental* plants and *edible* plants (vegetables and fruits). Ornamental plants are either floriculture plants or nursery plants. Floriculture plants, also called bedding plants, are flowers, grown for their blossoms, or foliage plants, grown for their showy leaves. Nursery plants, usually wood or perennials, are raised for landscape purposes.

These classifications are useful to people working in the field of landscaping and gardening because landscapers arrange plants according to their uses. This is not the same as scientific classification, which we will cover later.

Introduction to Botany

Both plants and animals are living organisms, and their basic life processes are very similar. The study of plants is called botany. The main difference between animal cells and plant cells is that plant cells have rigid cell walls and animal cells do not. Plant cell walls contain cellulose, which makes the plant cell rigid and gives it a definite shape. Cellulose is tough, flexible material. Wood is composed of cellulose that is impregnated with a special material called lignin, which provides rigidity and strength to the cellulose. Woody plants have a unique combination of both living and dead cells making up their stems.

Inside the cell wall is a jelly-like material, the protoplasm. The protoplasm is the living substance that is the basis of all life, in both plants and animals. Within the protoplasm is a small area of dense material called the nucleus. The nucleus controls the cell and its processes, as well as the

Division of Horticultural Plants

1. Types of Ornamental Plants and Examples

Floriculture Plants

Flowers and foliage plants

- Annuals
  petunia, marigold, zinnia
- Biennials
  hollyhock, foxglove
- Perennials
  peony, tulip, silver mound

Nursery Plants

- Lawn or turf plants
  Kentucky bluegrass, Bermuda grass
- Vines, woody and herbaceous
  wisteria, English ivy
- Ground cover
  sedum, ajuga, periwinkle
- Shrubs, evergreen and deciduous
  juniper, forsythia
- Trees, evergreen and deciduous
  blue spruce, pin oak

2. Edible Plants

Vegetables

Plants grown for above-ground portions

- Cole crops
  cabbage, cauliflower, broccoli
- Legumes
  beans, peas
- Solanaceous fruit crops
  eggplant, tomato, peppers
- Greens and salad crops
  spinach, lettuce, chard
- Vine crops
  cucumber, melon, squash
- Herbs and spices
  dill, spearmint, nutmeg
- Miscellaneous
  corn, asparagus

Plants grown for below-ground portions

- Tubers
  potato, yam, sunroot
- Bulbs
  onion, garlic
- Root crops
  carrot, radish, sweet potato

Fruits

Deciduous fruits

- Small fruits
  grape, strawberry, raspberry
- Tree fruits
  pear, apple
- Stone or drupes
  peach, apricot, plum
- Nuts
  walnut, pecan

Evergreen or tropical fruits

- Herbaceous perennials
  banana, pineapple
- Tree fruits
  orange, lemon, avocado, fig
- Nuts
  macadamia, cashew

form in which it develops. How plants take on specific characteristics that distinguish them from one another is the basis of the science of genetics. Genetics and heredity apply to both plants and animals in similar ways.

Cells also contain the chemicals that allow plants to grow and that keep them nourished and alive. Each cell respires, takes in nutrients, uses the nutrients to grow, and gives off waste materials. Although all cells are similar, cells can be different in their structure and function. Certain cells in every plant manufacture food for the plant. These cells are usually in the plant leaves. These cells contain chloroplasts in their protoplasm. Chloroplasts are usually green in color since they contain chlorophyll.

Chlorophyll is a chemical that uses sunlight, carbon dioxide from the air, water, and other nutrients to make the carbohydrates that the plant uses for energy. This food nourishes the plant and makes it grow. It is important to remember that the energy required to make plants function comes from the sun in the form of sunlight.

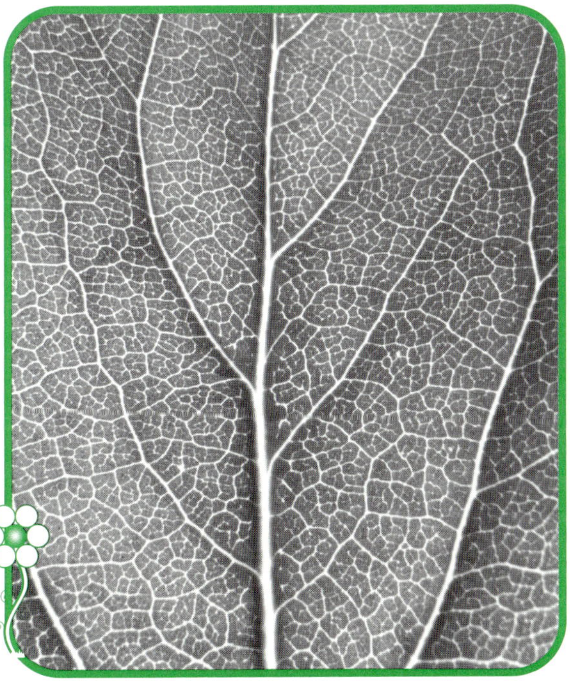

Another thing to know is that while animal life consumes oxygen and releases carbon dioxide, for plants it is mainly the opposite. Thus plants play a vital role in balancing the scale with animal life and keeping the earth's atmosphere stable. Without plants, animal life could not survive.

Food made in the leaves will not benefit the plant if it stays in the leaves. Just as animals have circulatory systems to transport blood throughout the body, plants also have a system that transports essential material. Plants have vascular systems made up of specialized tissues that transport material. The xylem transports water, and the phloem transports food made in the leaves.

We will discuss how plants make and transport food as we study roots, stems, leaves, and flowers. These parts may look very different in different types of plants, but they are found in all plants used in gardening and landscaping. Let us consider each one of these parts individually and study its function. This will help you understand how to care for the total plant.

Roots

Roots often make up about half the weight of the entire plant body. The major function of the roots is absorption of water and nutrients from the soil. Nutrients, which are mainly minerals, are dissolved in water and taken into the root. Another purpose of the root system is to anchor the plant. This is particularly important in large landscaping plants. There are two types of plant roots, taproots and fibrous roots. Taproots are deeper roots that provide better anchorage and a more reliable water supply.

Examples of plants with taproots are apple trees, walnut trees, carrots, and beets. Fibrous roots, common to grasses, are shallower compared to taproots. Fibrous-rooted plants and trees are more affected by drought conditions but respond quicker to fertilizers. It is important to note that no root system will grow deeper into the soil than available oxygen, water, and nutrients will allow.

Water is absorbed by root hairs, which are cells that line the outside of the roots. Root hairs can be damaged by dryness. This can reduce the amount of water the roots can absorb even after the plant is given water. Care must be taken not to damage the root hairs when transplanting or caring for plants.

Stems

All plants require food for growth and development. Food is manufactured by the chlorophyll in the leaves only when the leaves are exposed to light. It is advantageous to most plants to expose as much foliage to the sun as possible. Therefore, the stem functions to hold the leaves up to the sun.

Water and dissolved nutrients needed to make food are absorbed by root hairs, and then passed from xylem cell to xylem cell until they reach the leaves. Food produced in the leaves is again transported down to the roots and throughout the plant by the phloem, in a watery solution.

As mentioned earlier, horticultural plants are vascular plants. There are three types of vascular plants: ferns, cone-bearing plants, and flowering plants. Ferns are the simplest vascular plants since they do not produce seeds. The most important cone-bearing plants are conifers, which include the evergreen trees in the temperate zone (spruce, pine, fir, and hemlock). They produce their seeds in cones instead of flowers. Flowering plants are divided into two subclasses, monocotyledons and dicotyledons. These lengthy names are shortened to monocots and dicots.

An easy method of distinguishing between monocots and dicots is by the leaves. Monocots have parallel-veined leaves; dicots have netted-veined leaves. All grasses, lilies, orchids, irises, and palms are monocots. The term grasses, as used in horticulture, means more than the grass used on sod for lawns. Grasses refer to a whole family of plants that have narrow leaves, hollow stems, and flowers arranged on spikes. They include turf grasses (e.g., *Kentucky bluegrass*), ornamental grasses (e.g., *pampas grass*), grains (e.g., *wheat*), and bamboo. Most of the trees, shrubs, weeds, and familiar flowers not mentioned above are dicots.

Leaves

Most of the plants used in landscaping have thin, flat, green leaves that are well adapted to receive and use light. We have already pointed out that leaves are green because they contain chlorophyll, the chemical used in food manufacturing. Photosynthesis is the process of making food, which is the chief work of the leaves, using the sun's energy.

In addition to sunlight, photosynthesis also requires water, minerals (elements from the soil), and carbon dioxide. Water and minerals come from the soil and are absorbed by the roots. Carbon dioxide is a gas taken from the air by the leaves. The sugar produced in photosynthesis is converted into starches (complex carbohydrates) and fats (oils). Food is stored in plant roots, stems, and seeds. Both starches and fats may be converted back into sugars and used by the plants for energy, whenever it is needed.

Another interesting feature of plants is that they breathe much the same way animals do. The net result in plant breathing is that carbon dioxide is taken into the leaves and oxygen is given off. Leaves have small pores that allow gases to enter and exit. At the same time, they also allow some water vapor to escape from the plants. (Some plants can also take in water directly through the pores in the leaves, and not only through the roots.) Plants can lose a great amount of water through pores, particularly during hot and dry conditions, and you must be aware of this when working with plants. Plants will also lose water much more rapidly if the leaves and stems are cut or damaged, or if the roots become severed or exposed. Although plants need some water for photosynthesis, they have a greater and more urgent need of water to replace water losses.

Flowers

Many ornamental plants are grown for their showy flowers. Rhododendrons, roses, lilies, and tulips all have large, beautiful flowers. All monocots and dicots are flowering plants, and most do not have large, showy flowers. Although flowers are important in landscaping, they have another purpose besides beauty. Flowers produce seeds to reproduce the plant.

Flowers develop from buds on the plants' stems. On some plants, such as buddleia and hydrangea, flowering buds are only on the new season's growth, while other flower buds, such as those of forsythia and weigela, are only on older wood. This distinction is important because it determines the best time to prune the plants.

Flowers are stems and leaves that are adapted for reproductive purposes. We find flowers attractive and so do insects and birds, which help in seed production. Flowers from different types of plants look very different but have the same basic parts. The four main flower parts are petals, sepals, stamens, and pistils. Some flowers have one or more of these parts missing.

The petals are usually the colored parts of the flower, but not always. For example, the large red parts of the poinsettia are modified leaves called bracts. The true flowers are the unassuming parts in the center of the bract clusters. All the petals together are called the corolla.

The sepals enclose and protect the flower bud. They are usually the small, green, leaflike structures below the petals. The sepals are easy to find on flowers like the rose, since they are green. On other flowers, such as the orchid, tulip, lily, and cyclamen, they are the same color as the petals and more difficult to identify. They are still the outer layer of the bud. All the sepals together are called the calyx.

The stamens are the pollen-producing organs. They are made up of the anther and its stem, called the filament. When

the pollen is mature, it breaks through the anther wall.

The pistil is in the center of the flower and it consists of the stigma, the style, and the ovary. The stigma is the part that receives the pollen. It is usually a moist or sticky surface at the top of the pistil. The style is the tube that leads from the stigma to the ovary. The mature ovary, with or without seeds, becomes the fruit.

Pollen is usually a fine, yellow dust. Each grain is a male sex cell. The pollen is transferred to the stigma by wind, bees, or insects. The male cell moves down the style until it comes in contact with the egg cell in the ovary. There, fertilization occurs and seeds are produced.

There are some complete flowers with both the male and female parts. Then in other species there are male flowers (which have only stamens), and female flowers (which have only pistils). Some plants have both male and female flowers on the same plant; they are called monoecious plants. Other plants have separate male and female flowers; they are called dioecious plants.

Self-pollination occurs when the pollen from the same flower or different flowers of the same plant fertilizes the ovary. Cross-pollination occurs when pollen from different plants fertilize the ovary. When cross-pollination is needed to produce fruit, you must plant more than one tree or shrub for cross-pollination to occur. This is needed for many fruit trees, such as apple, and shrubs, such as holly and blueberry.

The receptacle is not a part of the flower, but it usually is the base where the flower is attached to the pedicel (also spelled pedicle), which is part of the stem. In many flowers, the ovary is contained with the receptacle, but in other flowers the ovary is mounted above the receptacle.

Plant Identification

Scientific Names

Plants have common names, as well as scientific names that are based on Latin words. Scientific names can seem cumbersome and difficult to remember when you first encounter them. However, there are advantages to identifying plants by their scientific names.

- Often there is more than one common name for plants. This can cause problems when gardening professionals order plant stock and discuss plants with customers. The scientific names are specific. You do not need to use the scientific names all the time, but there are times when it is good to check the information using scientific names.
- Scientific names are more systematic, and they tell you which plants are related. Since growing habits of related plants are often similar, you will learn more about plants if you know how they are related to one another.
- Scientific identification allows you to identify plants by looking at leaves, stems, flowers, and so on. If you know plants only by the flowers, your recognition skills are limited when plants are not blooming.

Common Names

All plants are given a scientific name soon after they are discovered. This scientific name is usually in Latin, and the same identical Latin name is used by botanists throughout the world. Therefore, when you write or say the name *Acer rubra*, every person who works with plants knows the exact plant you are talking about. *Acer rubra* is also called the red maple by most people in the North America.

The common name of a plant changes from one language to another. For example, in Spanish zinnia is called rascamoño. Also, plants acquire more than one common name. Sometimes they have a dozen — yes, even twenty or thirty common names — in various sections of the country.

The reverse situation also occurs where one common name may refer to any of a dozen different plants. Take the common name "mock orange." What is it? There are probably twenty or thirty plants that have been called mock orange in one place or another — but correctly, it belongs only to the genus *Philadelphus*. (You will learn shortly what a genus means.)

Some scientific names are the same as the common names. You may be surprised at how many scientific names you already know. Chrysanthemum, hydrangea, rhododendron, and camellia are just a few examples.

Do not try to memorize the scientific names of hundreds of plants. Start with common plants used in landscaping or gardening in your area. Slowly you will build up your vocabulary.

Scientific names consist of at least two names. The first name is the genus to which the plant belongs. The plants of the same genus are closely related. For example, all oak trees are in the same genus, *Quercus*. The scientific names of all oak trees begin with the name *Quercus*. The genus name is always capitalized and sometimes only the capitalized initial is used.

The second name is the species name (abbreviated sp.). The members of the same species are even more closely related to each other than members of the same genus. The species name is not capitalized. For example, white oak is named *Quercus alba*, red oak is *Quercus rubra*, and pin oak is *Quercus palustris*. Each of these names may be written with just the capital Q, as in *Q. alba*.

The third name, if one appears, is the varietal name (abbreviated var.). In the cases of natural varieties, it is a Latin name. If the plant variety was developed on purpose by plant breeders, then it is called cultivated variety or cultivar (abbreviated cv. or cvs.), and an English name is used. Some cultivars are given names as a type of trademark, and these are given in single quotation marks. Plant breeders have been very busy creating new cultivars.

An Example of Scientific and Common Names

Below we identify the various parts of a scientific name and also give the common name for this variety.

Scientific Name:
Juniperus chinensis var. Pfitzer

Genus Name:
Juniperus

Species Name:
chinensis

Varietal Name:
Pfitzer

Common Name:
Pfitzer juniper

A typical example of a three-word scientific name is *Viburnum plicatum tomentosum*, whose common name is doublefile viburnum. A typical example of a cultivar is *Prunus serrulata* 'Kwanzan,' which is commonly known as Kwanzan flowering cherry.

Guides with Plant Keys

Guides, also known as field guides, are books with plant keys used to identify plants. There are many guides available. Usually each guide is used to identify one or two general types of plants in a region. For example, you may use a guide to trees and shrubs in northeastern and central North America. The usual approach to the identification of a plant is by the leaves, or foliage. Since leaves come in a great many shapes, sizes, and arrangements, it gives us many identifiable parts.

Types of Leaves

To identify plants, first look at the basic types of leaves. Are the leaves needlelike, scale-like, or broad-leaved? Needlelike leaves or scale-like leaves are usually found on conifers. If the leaves are not needlelike or scale-like, they are broad-leaved.

If the leaves are broad, which is most common, look next at how the leaves are arranged on the stem. There are three basic ways leaves are arranged:

Alternate arrangement means the leaves are staggered along the stem.

Opposite arrangement means two leaves are attached to the stem directly across from each other. They seem to be in pairs.

Whorled arrangement is when several leaves are attached at the same point in a spiral-like pattern.

Leaf Division

The third step is to determine whether the leaf is simple or compound. The basic rule is that the simple leaf has only one leaf blade on its leafstalk, or petiole. A compound leaf has several distinct parts or leaflets on its leafstalk. Usually this is quite simple to determine, but there are some tricky cases.

Simple leaves always have a continuous leaf blade, even though the blade may have a complicated pattern. The edge of the leaf may be cut, but it will not be cut completely to the midrib (the central vein of the leaf).

Compound leaves have leaflets that are attached to a stalk, which is attached to the stem. The individual leaflets are separated from each other by a section of leafstalk.

There are several types of compound leaves, but two types are especially common.

Palmately compound leaves are attached together at one site.

Pinnately compound leaves are separately attached to the leafstalk.

Each leaflet may seem like a complete leaf. A clue to look for is a bud. A bud is a condensed shoot that contains an undeveloped leaf, leaf cluster, or flower. Buds are found only at the point where the petiole is attached to the stem.

Start at the outermost part of the leaf, and trace back until you find a bud. This is where the leaf starts. If there are several distinct parts or separate blades beyond that point, the leaf is compound. If there is one continuous blade, then the leaf is simple.

If the leaves are needlelike, they may be bundled in clusters, or fascicles. The number of needles in each fascicle will

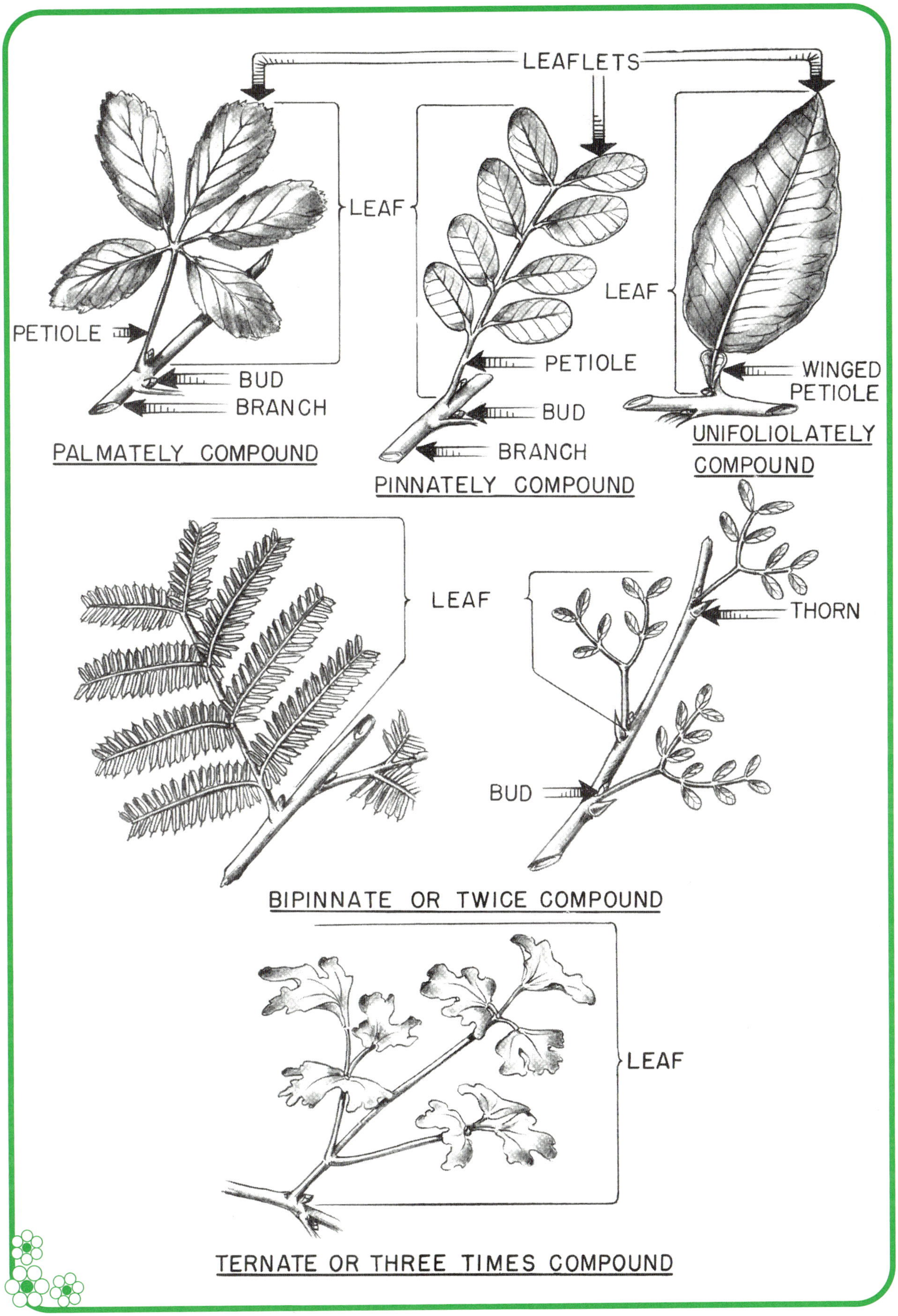
LEAFLETS
LEAF
PETIOLE
BUD
BRANCH
PALMATELY COMPOUND
LEAF
PETIOLE
BUD
BRANCH
PINNATELY COMPOUND
LEAF
WINGED PETIOLE
UNIFOLIOLATELY COMPOUND
LEAF
THORN
BUD
BIPINNATE OR TWICE COMPOUND
LEAF
TERNATE OR THREE TIMES COMPOUND

vary according to the type of plant. Pines have needles that are usually in fascicles. Firs and hemlocks have needles that grow separately along the stem. Remove a single needle and you will see a little round scar with a single dot in the center. Hemlock needles are usually shorter and flatter, with blunter ends than firs.

Arborvitae and junipers have scale-like leaves, which means that the needles are overlapping and pressed together, as in the figure below. In general, junipers have sharper scales and are prickly, whereas arborvitae are blunter with a smoother feel.

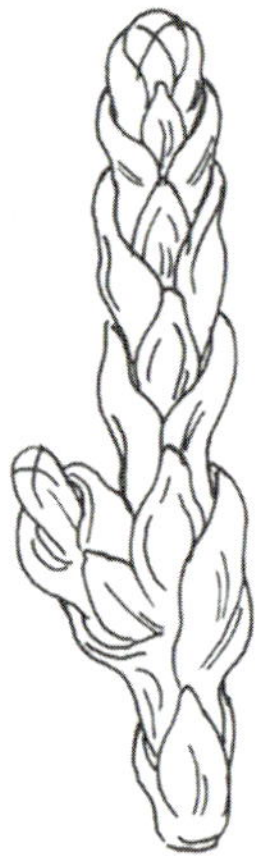

Scale-like leaves

Plant Key Divisions

Most field guides or other plant keys are divided into five basic sections based on what type of leaves a plant has:

- needlelike or scale-like leaves
- opposite compound leaves
- opposite simple leaves
- alternate compound leaves
- alternate simple leaves

Field guides that contain only flowers often are divided into flower colors, but most that identify trees and shrubs are organized according to leaf type. Check each book to completely understand how it works.

Leaf Venation

Once the general classification is determined, then other characteristics can be factored in. One characteristic is leaf vein patterns, or venation. There are three basic types of venation. In parallel venation, the veins run parallel to each other. This is commonly found in monocots. Net venation, common in dicots, is divided into two types, palmate and pinnate. Palmate ("like a hand") leaves have veins that come from one point at the leaf base, like fingers on a hand. Pinnate venation means "like a feather," and the side veins in these leaves branch off from a midrib.

Leaf Shape

Leaves come in various shapes. This characteristic is most interesting to study, and most of us know at least a few plants by the shape of the leaves. The long, heart-shaped leaf of the poplar, and the ribbonlike shape of the willow leaf are firmly imprinted on the minds of most plant lovers. Page 34 shows the many ways that leaf shapes may vary. Page 35 shows variations in leaf margins and the shapes at the bases and tips of leaves.

Leaf Venation

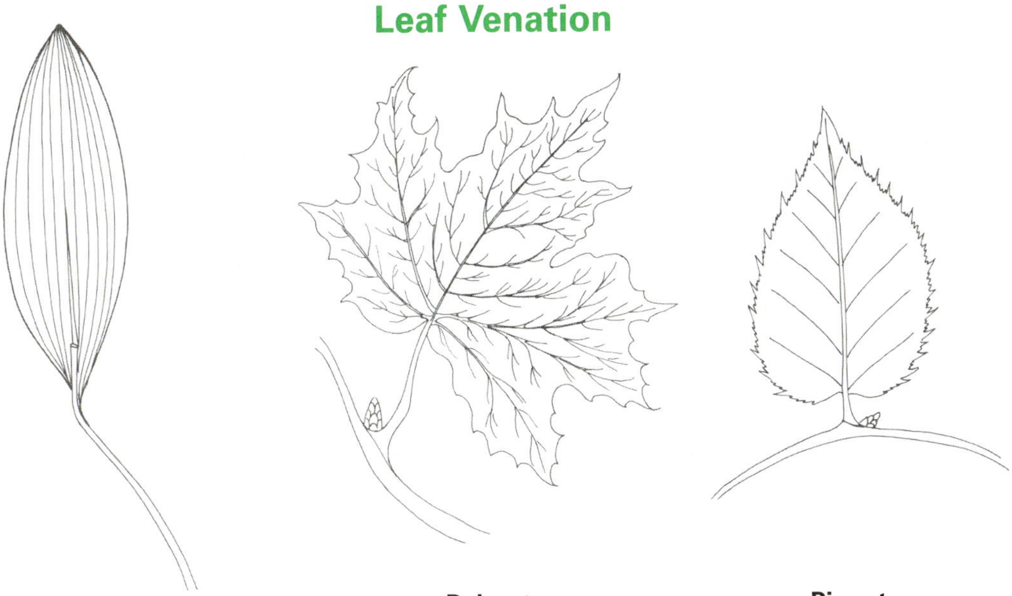

Leaf Texture

Texture of the leaf is also important. Some leaves feel leathery and coarse and others feel soft and finely textured. Some leaves have fine hairs that can be noticed only by touching the leaf. In some cases these fine hairs will be on only one side. Often there will be a marked color difference between the opposite faces of the leaf. Some leaves look glossy and others look dull.

Identifying Dormant Plants

Plants can also be identified when they are dormant. When dormant, deciduous plants have no leaves. One characteristic to look at in this case is the buds. Like leaves, buds are arranged either alternate or opposite from each other. The buds in the figure on page 36 are arranged alternately. Notice the buds, or groups of buds, at the ends of twigs or stems. Some plants never have more than one bud in this location, while others may have a group with possibly one in the group that is larger than the rest. This larger one is usually a flower bud. If we tear off the scales, the parts of the undeveloped flower will be found. Flower buds may also be found along the stem.

Two important things to look for when examining buds are their size and their shape. Are they large or small? Are they pointed, rounded, or oddly shaped? Also examine bud scales. Do the buds have numerous overlapping scales or just a single covering? Are the scales smooth and shiny, or are they covered with fine, soft hairs? These characteristics will help to identify plants.

Leaf scars are spots, usually below buds, where last year's leaves were attached to the plant. These scars have various shapes, but they will always have the same shape on the same type of plants. Therefore, we can use leaf scars to help us identify plants. Look

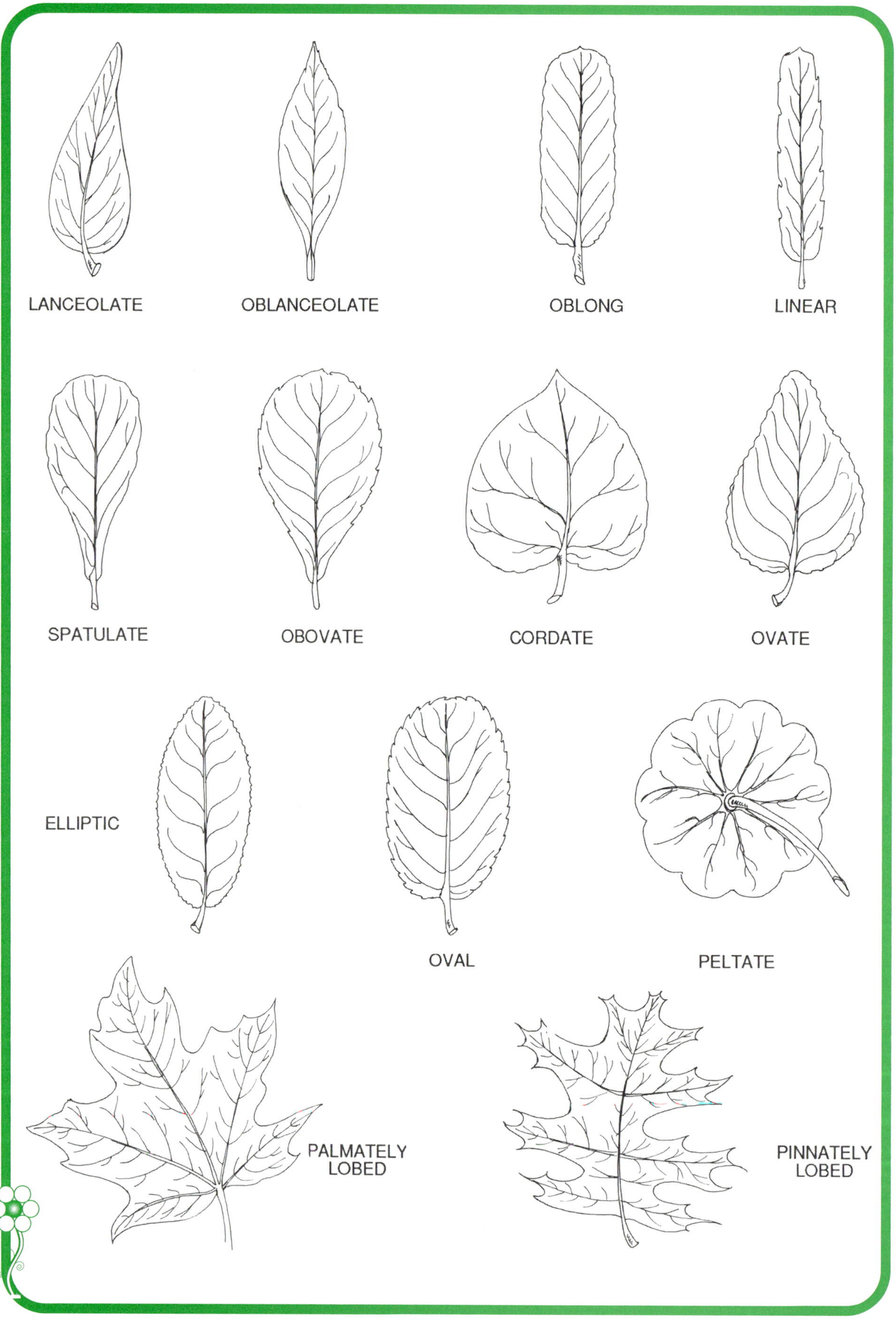
LANCEOLATE
OBLANCEOLATE
OBLONG
LINEAR
SPATULATE
OBOVATE
CORDATE
OVATE
ELLIPTIC
OVAL
PELTATE
PALMATELY LOBED
PINNATELY LOBED

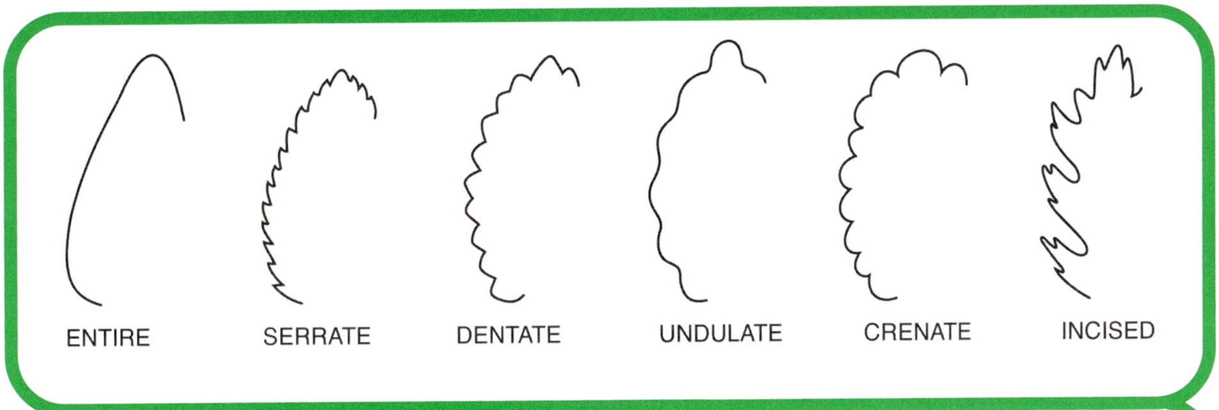
ENTIRE
SERRATE
DENTATE
UNDULATE
CRENATE
INCISED

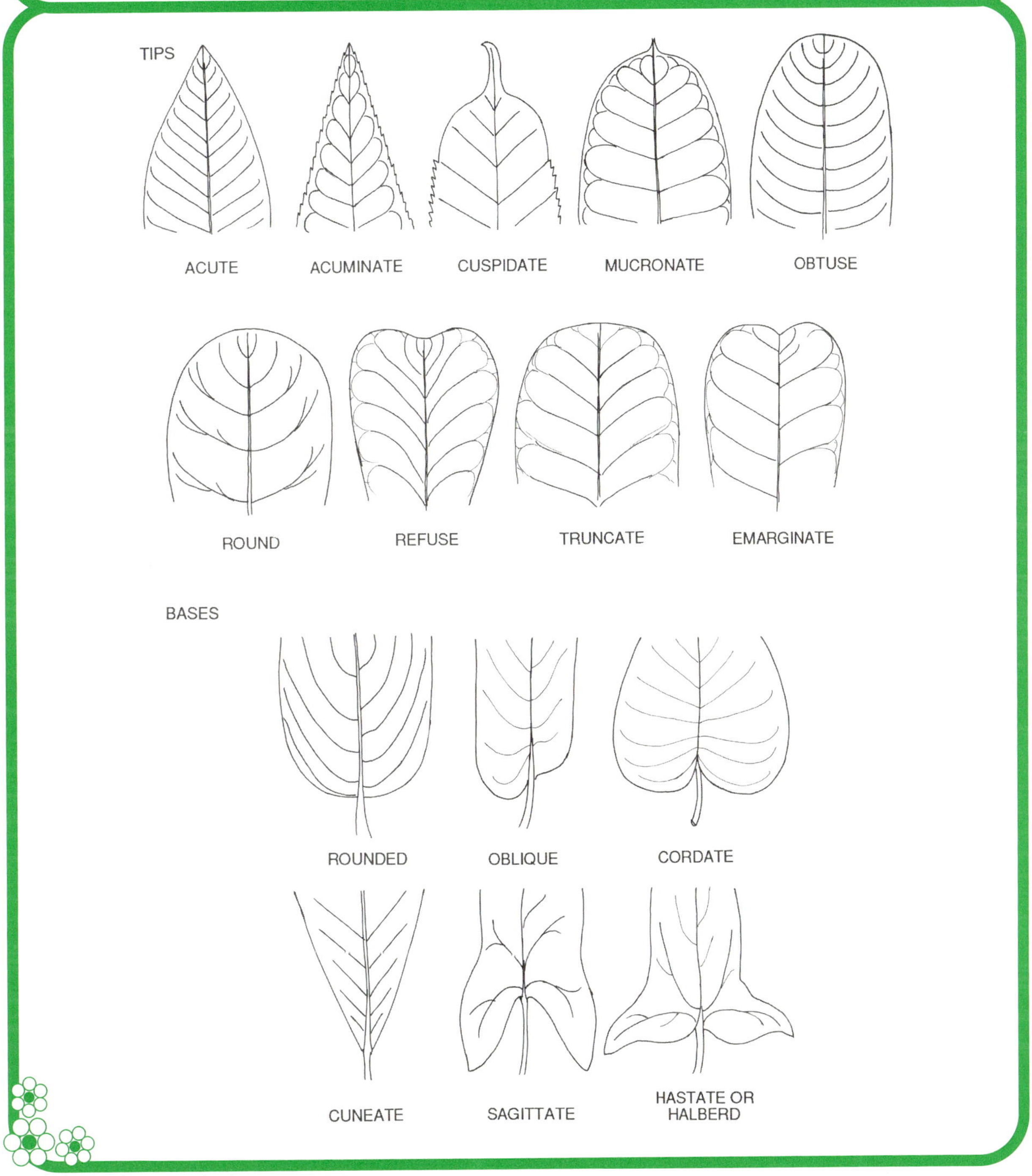
TIPS
ACUTE
ACUMINATE
CUSPIDATE
MUCRONATE
OBTUSE
ROUND
REFUSE
TRUNCATE
EMARGINATE
BASES
ROUNDED
OBLIQUE
CORDATE
CUNEATE
SAGITTATE
HASTATE OR
HALBERD

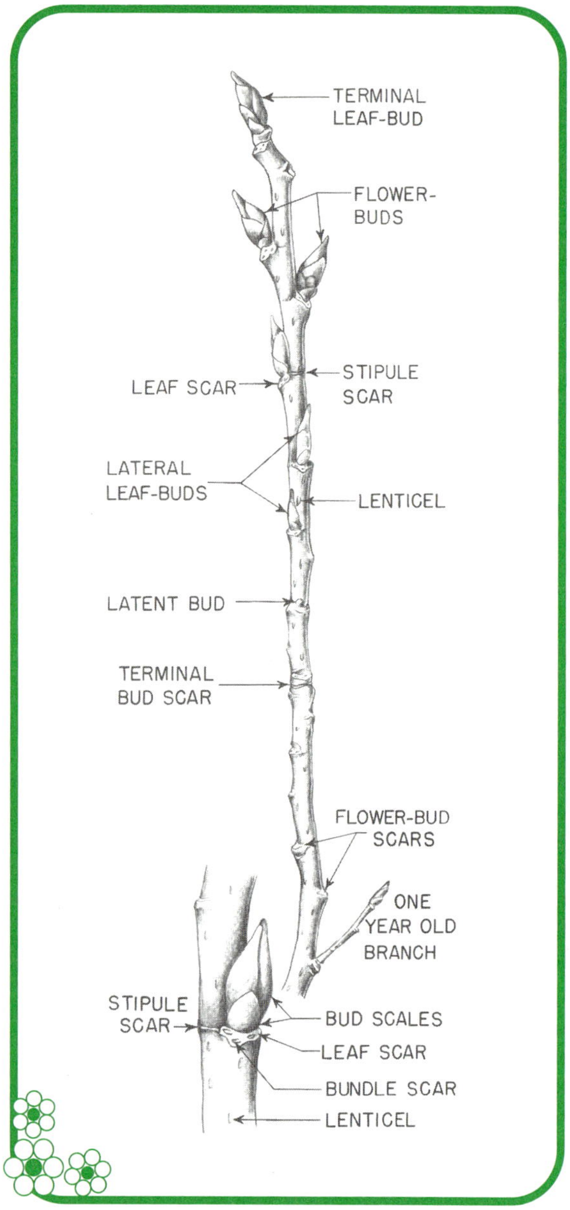

at these scars closely with a magnifying glass and you will see a definite pattern of small dots. These dots are called vascular bundle tips and are part of the vascular system that extends into the leaves.

Now look at the rest of the dormant twig. What type of surface does it have? Is the surface rough or smooth? Are there prominent lenticels? (Lenticels are small openings in the bark that permit gases to go in and out of the twigs. These are quite noticeable in birch and maple trees.) Does the plant have thorns? If so, where are they located and what is their shape? The color of the twigs is also important. Many dogwoods have brightly colored twigs and are easy to identify, if you know what to look for.

Sometimes it is necessary to observe more than the outside appearance of a plant to identify it. Several species of a plant genus may look so much alike that it is almost impossible to distinguish among them by outside appearance. When the twigs are split lengthwise, you will see that the pith is solid in some plants, in disk form in others, and in some it may be entirely lacking. However, it is always the same in like types of plants. Even the sap of a tree or shrub is worth noticing. Sap may be milky, as in sumacs. Other sap is sticky or watery, as in maples.

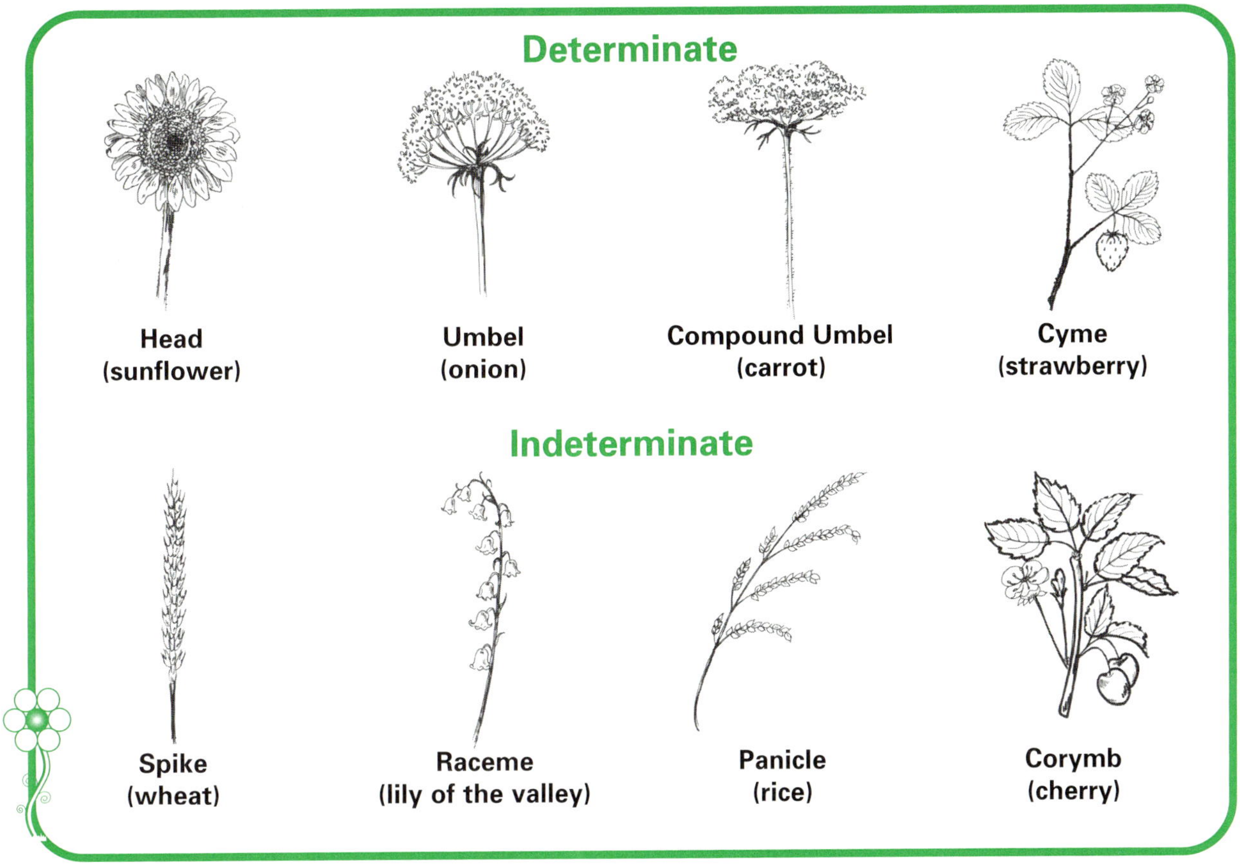

Identifying Flowers and Fruit

Flowers are very important features of floriculture plants. Some flowers are small and last only a short period of time, while other plants have large, showy flowers that bloom throughout the growing season. Identifying plants by their flowers is not always possible, since the plant must be blooming to use this method.

Earlier in this chapter we described the parts of flowers. For identification purposes, we are also concerned with the arrangement of flowers on the plant, or the inflorescence. The inflorescence can be determinate or indeterminate. Determinate inflorescence has a central or end flower that opens first so the axis, or flower stem, stops at that point. A head, or a single flower on a stem (like a sunflower), is determinate. An umbel is a determinate flower cluster, since it comes from a single point. An umbel can be rounded or flat, and simple or compound. A cyme is also determinate, but the flower cluster is branched instead of coming from a single point.

Flower clusters may also be indeterminate, which means that the primary axis continues to grow and develop flowers. A spike, which is an indeterminate inflorescence, has flowers along a main axis without branching. A shaft of wheat is a spike. A raceme has flowers along an axis, but the flowers are on small stalks. Lily of the valley is an example of a raceme. A panicle has several raceme-type branches. A corymb is also indeterminate, but it has flat-topped flowers, such as cherry.

Fruit can be used to identify plants. Botanically speaking, fruit is the mature ovary and other flower parts associated with it. It contains the seeds for reproduction of the plant. Seeds are also found in cone-bearing plants, which do not have flowers. There are many types of fruit, cones, and seeds used to identify plants.

Fleshy fruits are those most of us think of as fruit. Berries are fruits with many seeds, such as grapes, bananas, squash, and tomatoes. Drupes are fruits with one seed in the form of a stone. Plums, cherries, and peaches are examples of drupes. Pomes, such as apples, pears, and quince, are fruits that develop from flower parts besides the ovary. You find a core or papery tissue in pome fruits.

There are also dry fruits. Some dry fruits are in pods or capsules that open up when they mature to spread seed. Peas are in pods that open when mature. Jimson weed seeds are in a capsule that opens. Examples of plants with dry fruit that do not open when ripe are sunflower, corn, maple, oak, and walnut.

There are fruits that come from multiple flowers, such as pineapple, fig, and mulberry. Aggregate fruits are fruits that come from a flower with many pistils on one receptacle. They can have many stony seeds on a receptacle, like a blackberry, or they can have one seed on a receptacle, like a strawberry.

Conifers usually produce cones that can be used for identification. The scales on cones are closed until they become mature, when they open and spread the seeds. Each type of conifer has distinctive-looking cones. Yews and junipers are conifers that have berries instead of cones.

Garden Maintenance and Garden Features

Garden Maintenance

If we were going to study gardening and landscaping in the natural sequence of steps from the design and planning of a garden to its eventual routine maintenance once it is established, we would naturally start with design. However, sequential order isn't always the best way to learn a subject. Design and planning of a garden are among the most complex steps. This is because all of the latter stages, including maintenance, must be fully envisioned from the start in order for the design and the installation to be successful. Garden design and project planning are essentially management tasks, which most workers perform only after they have gained some experience.

There is another way that we can approach this extensive subject matter. We can use a different sequence: that of how new workers get started and are introduced to the workload. In almost every case, that means starting with garden and landscape maintenance. These are the tasks you need to understand well in order to land your first job in the field. Later, as you gain additional knowledge, you will get the chance to perform a wider range of tasks. Therefore, we will begin by running through everyday garden maintenance tasks.

Fertilizing

Fertilizing is a largely misunderstood activity. If it is done improperly, it will exacerbate the other maintenance problems in a garden.

By far the best time to add fertilizer to any garden is before planting. As part of the design process, it is very important to take soil samples to determine the general nutrient levels for a site. If the soil tests show that a deficiency exists, it is easy to add the needed fertilizer and rototill it into the soil prior to planting.

On the other hand, if there are already adequate nutrients in the soil, the addition of fertilizers will actually increase the plant s susceptibility to many insects and diseases. This is probably the most confusing aspect to the use of fertilizer, so it is worth explaining. If you have a plant growing on a site that has enough of every element needed for vigorous plant growth, it is possible to make the plant grow faster by adding more fertilizer. However, faster does not mean healthier! When plants are encouraged to grow more rapidly than normal, the cell walls of the new stems and leaves will be thinner than usual, which makes the plants prone to sucking insects such as aphids and scale, and to many leaf-destroying fungus problems.

All of this is not to say that plants should never be fertilized after they are installed in a landscape. However, fertilizer should be added only if there is a clearly identified element deficiency for a site. To determine the presence of a deficiency, it is necessary to perform a soil test. Soil testing kits are typically available from county extension agents and testing may be carried out by the state university or agricultural school in your area. As an alternative, there are many commercial soil laboratories, which may be found in your phone book. A few gardening professionals acquire the equipment and procedural know-how to perform the tests themselves.

For any of these options, it is first necessary to gather soil samples from the appropriate areas. If a lawn is being tested, gather small quantities (approximately one-half cup) of soil two to five inches from the surface (do not include the grass blades or roots) from about four to six scattered locations in the lawn. Put all of these samples together in a small bucket and stir the

samples to blend them. From this mixture, scoop out about one cup and place it in a bag to send to the soil lab.

For taking soil samples in landscape beds, it is necessary to gather samples that would represent the specific soil around the various types of plants that are present and to keep each of these samples separate. Do not include any of the mulch layers that may be present, but use the top two to five inches of soil under the mulch and gather about three-quarters of a cup of soil. Unless a shrub area is very large, it is not necessary to gather more than one soil sample for each plant type.

The soil testing lab will return the results, and this will direct you to apply specific amounts of fertilizer to correct deficiencies. The fertilizer should be applied to the soil surface and watered into the ground using irrigation. Past recommendations for drilling holes around trees and shrubs have been found to provide no advantage to the tree and may even damage roots. For trees and shrubs, the primary absorbing roots grow in the very surface of the soil, so there is no advantage to placing the fertilizers too deeply.

Pruning

Most plants that have been carefully selected for a site will need only minimal pruning. If a plant must be regularly pruned to control its size, it is recommended that the plant be replaced with one that is the appropriate size.

Pruning that is carried out in the garden or landscape should follow a certain protocol. This means that the first branches to be removed should be those that are completely dead. Dead branches are not only unsightly, but they also provide a place for diseases to get started in the plant. The second type of branches that should be removed are those that are damaged. These branches could have been damaged by weather, pests, or by some other injury. Damaged branches should be removed since they also provide a disease easy access to the plant. The third type of branches that should be removed are those that are crossing over other branches or are rubbing against other branches. And, finally,

you should make pruning cuts that will correct any faults to the plant form that were caused by the earlier pruning cuts.

It is important to note that pruning is not absolutely necessary for most plants in the landscape. Plants that are allowed to grow to their normal size and form have a far more interesting shape than plants that are constantly modified to have a different form. However, there are exceptions. To give one example, pruning is absolutely essential to get most fruit trees to produce large and attractive fruits, and to prevent limbs from becoming overloaded and breaking.

When pruning hedges, remember to occasionally cut out some sections of the plant to allow light to reach the interior branches of the plant. This will maintain its vigor and will result in a plant with better form.

Controlling Insect Damage and Diseases

Insect damage and diseases may be reduced and sometimes eliminated by careful design. During the design process, it is important to choose plants that will grow most vigorously with the site conditions that are present. If a plant is not able to tolerate the site easily, it will be much more susceptible to disease problems than another species that will grow vigorously.

Pest control has changed rapidly over the past twenty to thirty years. If we look back about 100 years, we find that most pest control was accomplished by pruning away diseased plants' parts or by using a variety of "home remedies" that often had undependable results. About midway through the twentieth century, there was a rapid increase in the availability of chemicals that provided excellent control for various pest problems. But by the late twentieth century, it became known that some of the common pesticides had undesirable side effects and so today our dependence upon these chemicals is changing.

The need for dependable pest control procedures has not diminished; however, the techniques used have been modified. It is now common for pest control to be implemented under what is called an Integrated Pest Management (IPM) program. An IPM program makes use of the least-toxic method of control available to the user. This means that an IPM program starts with good design so that only suitable plants are included in a landscape. After plants are installed, they are regularly monitored to check for the presence of possible disease problems.

By checking the plants regularly, it is possible to control pest problems at their earliest stage of development, sometimes by simply pruning out the problem area. If pruning does not appear to be an appropriate control, then low-toxicity pesticides are used to control a pest population while it is still small.

Under current laws in many areas, no fertilizer or pesticide may be commercially applied without the user holding a valid applicator's license from their state or provincial government. Applying any of these materials without a license could result in serious fines and possible imprisonment. To find the correct licensing procedure for your area, contact your county extension agent or your state or province's department of environmental protection. You should also be aware that there are often municipal bylaws prohibiting the use of certain chemicals, particularly in lawn care. This means that a chemical or practice that is permissible in one part of your state or province may not be in the specific place where you live. Thus, don't presume that simply because products are sold on shelves in nearby stores or garden centers that they are legal to use at a particular site.

Watering

Watering, as with fertilizers and pest control, is best dealt with as a design issue. If you have an area that is regularly very dry, it is strongly recommended that the primary plants of the landscape be plants that will tolerate the long periods of dry weather. Plants that do not get enough water are prone to pest problems and can greatly increase the cost of maintaining the landscape. Also note that in many parts of the country the public water supply is limited and irrigation is regulated by law, so you should become familiar with the water laws in your area.

At the time of installation, all landscapes will need some water until roots have grown to a sufficient size to support the plant. During this period of

establishment, it is important to know when and how much water to apply. First, there is no regular schedule that will work; you can't accurately predict that a plant will need water every day or every other day. It is important to supply water at the same rate the plant is using it. It is also important to apply the water in the location where the roots are able to absorb it. This means that, for very young plantings, you should apply water to the original root ball and to the area immediately outside of that ball.

Water is used by a plant in four primary ways:

1. It is used as a raw material in the photosynthetic process.
2. It is used as one of the primary components of each live plant cell.
3. It is used to transport sugars and elements throughout the plant.
4. It is used to cool the plant by evaporation from the plant's leaf surfaces.

Too much water is as damaging as too little water. If there is too much water in the soil, the plant will not be able to absorb it properly and the top of the plant will appear to wilt. This causes many people to add even more water until the plant finally drowns. To correctly time water application, it is necessary to monitor soil moisture. There are moisture meters available, but it is possible to get inaccurate readings with these devices. The best method for testing soil moisture is to use your finger as a probe. If a soil feels cool and moist to your finger, this is usually enough water for plant growth.

Mulching

Most plants will benefit from an appropriate layer of mulch over their root zone. The important thing to remember is not to make the depth too great. In recent years, many people have begun to build mountains of mulch at the base of their trees. These deep layers of mulch are causing major damage to the trunks of the trees and will encourage a variety of bark-destroying pests.

An appropriate layer of mulch will be not more than two to three inches in depth and will have no depth at the root flare of the tree. The mulch should be of a coarse texture to provide the best possible aeration and moisture movement. The use of finely textured mulch is not recommended.

Mulch used for annual flower beds should be chosen carefully. Some hardwood bark mulches may cause damage to annual flowers, so their use should be carefully considered.

Edging and Cultivating

Edging beds (cutting straight lines at the edges) is an activity that should occur about every two years to maintain a neat appearance with neat lines. In the southern states, this may need to be done annually since the lawn grasses grow more vigorously. There are many edging materials available that limit the introduction of grass into a bed, but their use should be a design decision.

Cultivation in a planting bed should not be a regular activity. Cultivation has been used to reduce populations of weeds, but it has been found that regular cultivation causes excessive damage to the absorbing roots of wood plants. Therefore, weed control should be addressed at the time of plant installation and be maintained through the use of proper mulching techniques.

Staking

Staking to maintain the appearance of a perennial garden should be done using a minimum number of stakes. It is best if the stake used is not taller than the plant and is a green color to camouflage its appearance. The material used to tie up the plant is best if it is a biodegradable string of a light brown color.

Other than temporary staking of perennial plants, no other staking is recommended for most flower and shrubbery gardens. However, certain fruits and vegetables should be staked to keep the fruit off the ground and to prevent heavily loaded branches from breaking. Staking may also be advisable in particularly windy locations or to protect certain prized plants from an impending storm. Also, stakes are sometimes used along with trellises or pieces of fencing to allow plants with a climbing habit to have something to attach themselves to as they climb.

Winter Protection

If a plant requires winter protection, its use in the landscape should be seriously questioned. Plants that are unable to survive winter conditions on their own will be much more susceptible to pest problems than will cold-tolerant plants. Of course, as always when it comes to gardening rules, there are a few exceptions. Some plants are tolerant to cold temperatures, but may need some protection from severe winter winds, ice, or heavy snow loads.

If a person wants to grow a plant out of its normal zone for special interest, there are some basic principles that must be observed. Never wrap a plant with plastic sheeting, especially clear plastic, as this will greatly increase the temperature of the plant's crown and may kill the plant. A winter wrap should not be placed around a plant until it has gone dormant for the year and the ground has had a frost. The purpose of the wrapping is not to prevent freezing, but instead to prevent rapid freezing and thawing of the ground and to reduce the air flow around the plant (to prevent drying of the plant).

The best material to use for wrapping such a plant is tightly woven burlap cloth. The burlap should be attached to stakes that are about four to six inches away from any part of the plant and should be taller than the plant.

If you wish to protect a plant from excessive snow loads, build an open

lattice structure, 1 foot above the plant, that is sturdy enough to support anticipated snows for the area. The lattice should have openings that are about 1½ to 2 inches across to allow for good air flow. Tightly wrapping a plant with rope to prevent snow and ice damage often leads to damage or total loss of the plant.

Garden Structures and Features

As we continue to introduce you to the basic ingredients of gardening and landscaping, it is time now to survey the elements of a garden other than the plants. In the terminology of the trade, they are generally classified as garden structures and garden features.

Garden *structures* are generally considered to be any man-made objects in the landscape that are used for practical or structural purposes. Retaining walls, fences, and garden houses are examples.

Garden *features* are somewhat different in that usually they are used for interest or aesthetic reasons. An object could, however, be both a structure and a feature. There is no hard and fast line that distinguishes between them. The appropriate use of garden features can add interest to many gardens and landscaped areas.

Precautions for Garden Feature Selection

Although the use of garden features should be encouraged, it is also important to note that great care and thought are required to avoid many of the pitfalls that result from poor design. Including a statue or other feature without creating a sense of purpose for the feature and at least some small degree of originality can result in clutter in the landscape. The use of mass-produced concrete or plastic animals within a plan seldom adds value to the landscape and should be avoided. Garden archways or trellises that are of poor design or that do not appear to fit into the overall plan should also be avoided. Sundials and bird baths are often overused, but if they are of good design and positioned properly, they will probably prove to be an asset in the garden.

In general, landscapers should be very selective and cautious when it comes to adding features. Only a small number of quality, tasteful features should be considered.

Landscape designers usually have contacts among specialty sellers of home and garden fixtures and unique design elements, as well as artisans

who are able to do custom work. Professionals also understand that there can be too much of a good thing, and that exotic looking features should be used sparingly, if at all.

Present-day gardens are often designed to be attractive without features. The present trend in garden design is toward a greater use of architectural structures. In the best of modern gardens, features, structures, design, and livability all blend into one harmonious picture.

Patios, Terraces, and Decks

There isn't a great deal of difference between a patio and a terrace. Technically, a patio is generally considered to be a partially or entirely enclosed terrace. In other words, a patio is more apt to be surrounded by the walls of the house, by garden walls, or by combinations of house and garden walls. The terrace is more open, usually adjoining one wall of the house and opening up into the general garden area.

A deck combines many of the design elements for both patios and terraces. However, a deck has the additional factor of being located above the grade of the surrounding landscape.

In present-day garden design, there is often a need for a patio, terrace, or deck to serve as a connecting link between the interior and exterior living spaces. Which of these elements to use depends upon the architectural style of the home and the needs of the users of the landscape. This connecting link is extremely important, and functionality is the key issue. You need to examine the lifestyle of the homeowner and determine what uses will be made of the backyard and patio area, and how many people it must be able to accommodate at any given time. The size of such an area should also be such that it bears a pleasing relationship to the size of the garden and to the house.

Many garden structures are far too small. The reason for this may be cost, but it is also often the result of not recognizing the needs of the users. Typically, the space should be at least nine square feet for each of the intended users of the space. Typically, this will mean an area about the same size as the living room for the house. This is reasonable since similar uses could be envisioned for these two spaces. This is particularly true these days, since a well-equipped terrace has almost as much furniture as the living room.

The proportions of the space are also very important. The garden structure needs to reflect the sense of space found in the house. Long, narrow forms will feel like a hallway and are usually of less value than a more rectangular form.

The structure need not be a specific geometric form. Its shape should be one that fits in with the overall design of the house and garden. In other words, the structure should be designed to be part of the whole.

In practice, landscapers often find a structure already existing, placed by an architect or builder who gave no thought to its relationship to the garden. These existing structures are often a real problem for the garden designer. Sometimes they are just plain impossible, and the best advice one can give the homeowner is to remove them and start over.

Concrete is the most commonly used material for garden terraces, but it is seldom the most attractive. However, it can be used effectively. Exposing the aggregate (hard matter in the concrete) is one method to improve concrete's appearance. Breaking the concrete into patterns with wood dividers is another. Brick and stone are also effective surfacing materials.

When working with existing decks, carefully check the wood of the deck for signs of decay or weak components. Typically, treated lumber should be used for the structural elements of a deck, but either redwood or cedar may have been used for the decking and railing parts. Although all of these materials have demonstrated excellent durability, any of them may eventually fail. Too many people overestimate the effectiveness of pressure-treating wood in preventing rot. Additionally, because pressure-treated wood often contains arsenic it is not suitable for use in play areas for children, and more and more localities are restricting its use elsewhere as well. This isn't a huge problem, because there are some premium "water seal" products that can be used to coat wood and that are far better at preserving it. However, be aware that water-sealed wood is often slippery when wet, so add materials or preparations to increase traction in areas that are used heavily and on any stairs or inclined wooden surfaces.

Fences and Walls

Fences are usually enclosures or barriers, or are added for decorative purposes. Walls are usually used for protection or to retain the soil. Walls are of heavier materials (such as stone or brick) than the materials used for fences. Wall construction is an advanced topic and one best left to specialists. Small mistakes in the design or installation of a wall can cause it to shift, crack, or collapse over time.

If the purpose of a fence is entirely practical, a simple wire fence may be sufficient to provide enclosure. The landscape designer should be careful not to spend large sums of money for an ornate fence that will, in a year or two, be covered or hidden with plant foliage.

Fences should be built to reflect the architectural qualities of the home. If a house is built in a Victorian style, fencing should carry details that are typical for that period of architecture. When designing a fence, keep your mind set on what will be needed to maintain the structure, as this could be a burden to the owner. Painted wood needs to be scraped and repainted often, and paint is poor at protecting wood from rotting. Stains and sealants are more effective and more durable. They also tend to give a more natural look.

When using quality wood made of whole boards (not plywood or particle board), enhancing the natural wood grain, rather than hiding it, gives a more natural and earthy feel that often works well with the rest of the garden design. However, if cheaper grades of wood are used, they will need to be painted, covered with a veneer, or otherwise concealed. This will often mean a shorter life and higher maintenance needs. Cheap wood is usually no bargain in the long run.

One simple type of fence now used extensively is constructed of cedar or redwood palings (stakes or pickets). Such a fence affords excellent screening, and the upkeep is negligible, because it is most often left untreated. The wood weathers and soon blends with plantings, giving a pleasant mellowed effect.

In all wood fence construction, avoid as much contact as possible between the wood and ground. A clearance of at least two inches is desirable. Posts can also be set above ground by use of the method illustrated in the figure below. It is usually not necessary to set posts into concrete, and doing so may decrease the life of the post. As the wood of the post expands and contracts with its moisture content, the wood is damaged at the surface of the concrete. Therefore, if concrete is to be used, the posts should be attached to metal brackets, or plates, that are set into concrete, as shown below.

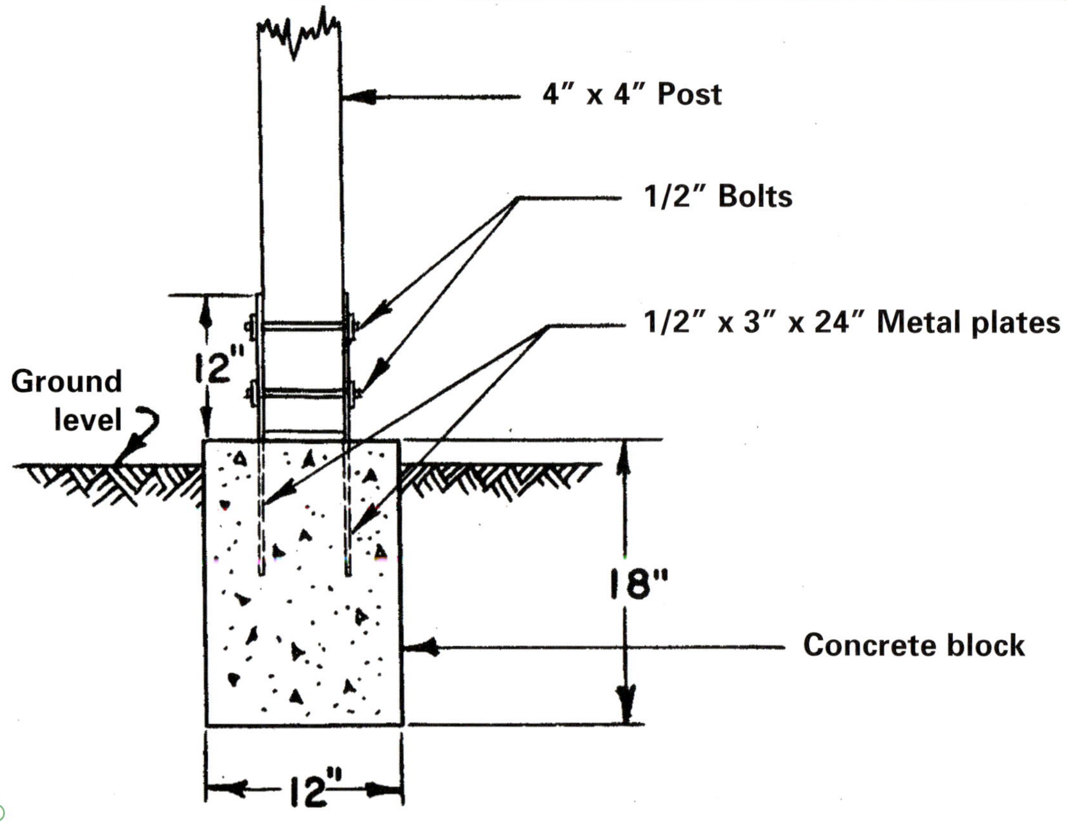

Posts should be set to a depth that will allow for long-term stability. In many locations, it will be necessary to dig to below the frost line of the soil. Posts that are used to support the added weight of the gate should be dug to a greater depth, and it is often necessary to use concrete to make the gateposts more stable. In this situation, the surface of the concrete should be several inches below grade to lessen the chance of damage caused by expansion of the wood. All other posts should be set in place by firmly stamping the original soil into the hole around the posts.

Gateways

Gateways are usually built in conjunction with a fence. Everything said regarding the fence applies equally to gateways.

Gateways can be charming and add curiosity. Everyone likes to see what is on the other side of an attractive feature of this type, and this helps to give interest to the garden. A gate also enhances the effect that one is entering a private garden that not everyone has a chance to see.

Benches and Seats

Undoubtedly, more gardens should be equipped with well-placed garden seats. Far too many gardens never provide a visitor or an owner a chance to rest and enjoy the garden.

Seats may be placed on the border of the lawn or along walks, backed perhaps by shrub plantings, or they may be used in the shade area beneath a tree. These features may be of stone, wood, or concrete. In some sections of the country, very clever cement work is being done that is an excellent imitation of stonework. However, stone or concrete has the disadvantage of being rather cold, uncomfortable, and hard to sit on.

Bird Features

There are two types of bird features: those that are purely decorative and those that are actually intended to attract birds by providing nesting and feeding sites. If the property owner wants the latter type, some research must be done into the types of birds apt to be attracted to the site, or that the owner wishes to attract, and the features must be designed accordingly. Avoid the many poorly designed bird feeders on the market. For example, in most hummingbird feeders the artificial nectar can become rancid and attract hornets. Some seed feeders allow seed to become contaminated or get wet and moldy. A professional must know how to achieve proper results.

Bat houses are also becoming increasingly popular in some parts of North America where bats are plentiful. Bats are extremely beneficial because at night they consume large quantities of mosquitoes. However, some people dislike or fear bats, so you should not suggest this option unless the owner has a particular interest in it. As with birdhouses that are intended to be functional and not just decorative, you must do the research and know what you are doing before setting up such a structure.

Barbecues

Barbecues can hardly be called garden features in the usual sense of using a feature for an ornament. The barbecue should, if possible, be used in an area by itself; if this is not possible, it should be placed where it is not too conspicuous.

The designer should be certain that the client requires a built-in barbecue. If it is to be used only a few times a year, the expense will not be justified, nor should the area required be sacrificed for this purpose. Good portable barbecues are available that will serve most homeowners' requirements.

Sloping Lots

Some of the most interesting landscape developments are those designed for hillside or sloping lots. A level lot is usually less expensive to develop, but seldom can the one-level garden compete for interest with one that is built on several levels.

When there is a change of levels, we almost always need walls and steps. Walls may be constructed of many

materials, and may serve various purposes. Even on level lots, a freestanding wall may be used to give privacy and seclusion to the garden area. However, the cost here is so much greater than for a fence that walls of this type are not as common as in the past, when materials and labor were cheaper.

Sloping lots can be picturesque, but they can also create serious water and drainage problems. More will be said about this in chapter 5.

Water Features

Water features are perhaps the most interesting objects to be found in gardens. There is something in the rippling of water akin to flames in the fireplace — something peaceful and restful, yet stimulating.

Pools come in many different sizes and shapes. The ones we will discuss here are purely decorative and not overly large. Large water features are not only expensive, but they required specialized engineering expertise equivalent to that needed when installing an inground swimming pool.

In designing a small decorative pool, we must first have in mind the type — formal or informal — that we wish to use. With this in mind, we must choose a suitable location with adequate sunlight. The location will dictate not only the size, but also the elevation of the pool, which in turn determines the grading of the area around the pool.

The location is of special importance if it is to be a natural pool with irregular earth and stonework. If a formal or geometric type is chosen, it must have the same scale, proportions, and character of the surrounding garden or area.

When establishing a location for a pool, the background should be considered. A satisfactory result will depend to a large extent upon the background; consequently, it should be carefully planned as a definite unit of the entire composition. If a pool is located in the center of a formal garden or lawn, it is very important to give it suitable surroundings. Quite often the effect of a pool or basin is lost when you look beyond it to an undeveloped area on the same or an adjacent property. Service poles, garages, or other service buildings in the background can detract from the attractiveness of a water feature.

The best background is a permanent one; permanent in winter as well as in summer. Plantings of shrubs and small trees form one of the best backgrounds for the informal pool.

It is important that almost any water feature be designed with some form of water circulation. This prevents stagnation and the breeding of mosquitoes. It also usually makes it unnecessary to chlorinate or treat the water, as one would have to do in a pool used for swimming. Allowing water to bubble or dribble or tumble down a slope causes oxygen to become dissolved in water, which can keep it clean enough for the purposes of a decorative garden. It also gives the water features a pleasing sound that can be as appealing as the visual effect. Achieving this generally requires the use of some sort of pump that is specially designed for this sort of outdoor use. It's worth spending a few extra dollars on a higher-quality and more rugged "pond pump" than what you would typically find at an average department store. Be aware that there are important electrical codes and safety issues regarding the circuitry for an outdoor electrical pump. You need to inform yourself thoroughly on these issues before proposing a pump installation in a garden design.

Formal plans should be drawn after the location and size of the pool and the type of the background have been determined. Plans help make construction of the pool more orderly and efficient. The plans will, of course, show the plumbing and the exact position of the supply lines and drains. The plans will also show the area and depth of excavation, as well as the area and depth of the gravel foundation. They should also show how forms are to be built and placed, and how the reinforcing soil is to be positioned.

Construction methods for pools and ponds are complex. They also vary significantly depending on the size and shape of the water features and the nature of the site. These days, even many large pools are likely to be purchased premolded in one piece, often with walls of fiberglass. If this is the case, the most essential part of the installation is preparing a bed to fit and fully support the pool all around, with minimal risk that the ground will shift after installation. However, preformed pools are not always suitable or desirable. The alternative is to have the pool entirely constructed on-site from poured concrete by a company that specializes in this work. The preparation steps are considerably more detailed in this case. The pool installer is responsible for the integrity of the installation, so his suggestions regarding the specific proposed plan should be carefully considered.

Pools may also be free-formed using a variety of rubber and vinyl liners. When using these materials, be sure that the chosen material will provide the intended service. Rubber roofing can be used, but this material often releases chemicals into the water that are toxic to fish and plant materials. Polyethylene plastic is not recommended for permanent features since this material is not usually stable in sunlight and is easily punctured. There are many vinyl liners made specifically for water gardens, and it is worth the effort to find these liners for a pool.

The advantages to using a sheet liner for a pool are that the pool is typically less expensive to install than concrete, the form is limited only by your imagination, a special form is not typically needed for installation, and, should it become necessary, modifying the size and shape of the pool is relatively easy to accomplish.

Caring for Plants in Water Features

Allow at least a month before placing fish or plants in a concrete pool. Up until this time the alkali in the cement will be toxic.

Pool water may become a greenish color due to algae. The algae can be killed by using 1 teaspoon of a saturated solution of copper sulfate (blue vitriol) or 2 to 4 teaspoons of saturated solution of permanganate of potash to each 13 cubic feet of water. However, be aware that these chemicals are toxic to fish and possibly to other creatures that may drink from the pool. The best way to control algae is to prevent too much direct sunlight from reaching it, and to add algae-eating fish and snails.

Water lilies are the most common pool plants. These should have an area of 10 to 25 square feet. They should be planted with their crowns 6" to 8" below the water's surface. Their roots require 8" to 12" of well-fertilized loam. Getting lilies to become well anchored can be difficult in some pools, especially where you are not able to establish enough soil on the bottom. One trick is to plant the roots and tubers of the lilies or other water plants in amply sized porous plastic containers or clear plastic bags full of rich organic soil, add a few stones for weight, and then seal or tie off the containers or bags except where the stems emerge. These can then be dropped into the pool, and enough dirt or stones pulled up around them to conceal the containers. One advantage of this approach is the containers can later be retrieved and brought inside and kept in an aquarium if the plants are not able to withstand winter conditions.

Some water plants are too delicate and fussy for certain locations and situations. The best solution, if you have the means to do so, is to start with species that are native to your area. These can be dug from shallow areas on the edges of ponds and transplanted.

Many species of lilies have a large and somewhat ugly-looking mass growing below the surface of the pond bottom, covered in rootlets and flattened protrusions that resemble eyes or leaf scars. These transplant well. In fact, sometimes they will resprout even if they are damaged or incomplete. This is one way these plants propagate in the wild. However, be aware that in some jurisdictions wetlands and water plants may be protected by law, especially on public land. If you are unable to dig up water plants legally yourself, try to obtain them from local growers. The point is that whenever it is possible to obtain them legally, local water plants do better than many exotic imports.

Walks, Roads, and Pavements

Circulation, or the ability to get from one place to another, is an extremely important consideration. No less important is the way we design and construct the walks and drives that make satisfactory circulation possible.

On many home grounds this basic rule has been given little consideration by the planner. This is unfortunate, for well-planned walks and drives immediately distinguish a garden.

The first consideration in planning walks and driveways is that they must be practical. Walks that need accommodate only one person at a time may be 18" to 24" in width, but where it is likely that two people may be walking side by side, or people will be passing each other, a 42" to 48" width is a minimum requirement. Remember, of course, that walks must be in scale with the area in which they are to be used, at least from a purely aesthetic standpoint. This will often modify practical considerations.

There are many types of materials that may be used for walks. We will briefly survey some of the possibilities.

Concrete Walks

Concrete has the advantages of long life and low upkeep. Its great disadvantage for garden purposes is that it has little, if any, aesthetic appeal in the way it is normally used. Its hard and uninviting surface, its stiff lines, and its gray color do not blend with the naturalness of plants and gardens. However, it can be made quite pleasing in appearance and satisfactory for garden purposes through the use of a textured surface or by exposing the aggregate. It takes considerable labor to obtain these pleasing surfaces, but they are well worth the extra effort.

Brick Walks

Bricks are a wonderful material for garden walks, for they lend themselves to a wide variety of uses and, if laid properly, always give an attractive result.

Brick walks may be laid either with or without mortar joints. It should be noted that the brick surface does not support the load of the walk, so special care should be taken in the construction of the base under the bricks.

A poorly laid brick walk can be a disaster. It may crack apart, or individual bricks may shift or be heaved upward by settling of the bed or by frost, creating tripping hazards. Many unmortared brick walks have been laid onto a sand base, but these walks tend to fail after only a few years. It is far better to lay the walk onto a base of gravel that has small stones or pebbles 1/4" to 3/8" in size. The gravel base provides excellent drainage that is needed for the long-term stability of the walk.

In unmortared brick walks, grass may start to grow between the bricks. Some people like this effect. It tends to soften the appearance of the walks and produces quite an informal feeling. However, some maintenance will be required, either to keep the grass clipped or to occasionally remove it with an adz (a tool to remove surplus material) when it becomes overgrown. To prevent grass from growing at all, one option is to chemically treat the soil in the walk area before laying the brick. A weed killer that kills all growth would be the type to use for this purpose.

Flagstone Walks

Flagstones of the right type make very pleasing garden walks. They are quite informal, more so even than brick, and appear natural.

When flagstone is used, it should have a good even surface; otherwise, it may be disagreeable to walk on. The stone should be 2" to 2½" thick. Flagstone

walks may be constructed in the same manner as brick walks. It is more difficult with flagstone, however, to obtain pleasing patterns, so it is best to employ the services of a professional stonemason. As with any walk, one made of flagstone should have parallel and straight sides. Care should be taken to see that joints are not continued from one row to another, as this becomes quite displeasing to the eye.

Stepping Stones

Another use of flagstone is for stepping stones. While this should seemingly be the easiest type of walk to put down, it can actually be quite challenging to do properly. A good stepping-stone walk is a rarity. First of all, it is difficult to determine the spacing of stones. People vary so much in length of stride that an average spacing will not suit everyone. There is only one way of getting around this, and that is to place the stones relatively close together and use good-sized stones. Stepping stones can be quite pleasing in a garden, but keep in mind that they are for locations where traffic is light.

Gravel or Decomposed Granite

Gravel walks are usually constructed with a 5" or 6" base of coarse material, and surfaced with 2" of fine pea gravel. With this type of walk, some type of curb is essential. Bricks on end can make a satisfactory curb. Concrete curbs may also be used. Where decomposed granite is available, a very inexpensive and quite presentable walk may be made by tamping down 3" of this material.

Grass Walks

In gardens where traffic is not too heavy, a simple grass path may be the best solution to circulation problems. Quite often, hard-surfaced walks do not blend into the garden scheme.

The use of grass walks depends somewhat on existing climatic conditions. If there are frequent heavy dews and the grass is usually wet, then such walks are not satisfactory.

It is essential, in any case, that these walks have a well-drained soil beneath them. An artificial-tile drain is usually desirable. If moisture does not drain from these areas rapidly, the grass will quickly be trampled, even by light traffic.

Patios and Large Areas

As previously mentioned, the general construction principles outlined for walks also apply to construction of patios. There are a few special situations, however.

If a patio or terrace is adjacent to a house and is to be underlain with a concrete base, the base of the patio should not be tied to the foundation of the house in any fashion. It is important that these two structures have a slight separation between them. The patio must have its own separate foundation to carry its load.

A footing is required all around the perimeter of the patio or terrace. The depth of such a footing will depend on climatic conditions. It should be well below the frost line. In warmer climates, a footing 12" wide and 6" deep is sufficient.

Irregularities in the surface of a large paved area are highly noticeable. Care should be taken to see that these irregularities do not occur.

Selecting and Using Plants in Landscape and Garden Design

Trees

Trees are the largest plants in a design and their placement is obviously important. Trees are used for specific reasons and functions. The primary reasons trees are used in a design are:

- **For shade**
- **For background**
- **As specimen trees**
- **As street trees**
- **For fruit**

Let's take a brief look at what we mean by each of these distinctions.

Trees for Shade

Any tree will provide a certain amount of shade. Most shade trees are planted fairly close to the home and should have branches that are rather high from the ground. Shade trees should shade a portion of the house, but not exclude light and air. They can also be used to frame the house for design purposes. Light, airy, open trees are better suited to be used near the house than the heavy, dense types. The latter tend to hide rather than complement the home.

In warmer climates, it is of course possible to use broad-leaved evergreen trees for shade year-round. You must ask yourself, and the homeowner, how much shade is needed. Deciduous trees will give you protection from the summer sun, and when the foliage is gone you will receive the benefit of the winter sun.

Before you decide to place any tree close to a home or other building, you need to consider its size and its habit (general shape and form) once it is mature. Will it tower over the house and look out of scale? Will it thrust against the house any branches that will constantly need to be cut back? Will it grow into electrical wires, and if so, will you be able to trim it away from the wires without creating a stunted and deformed shape?

You also need to consider the lifespan of the tree and its durability in the area. Birches grow faster than oaks and maples, but don't live as long or achieve the same stature. Some hardwoods are sturdier than others, less resistant to disease, and less prone to having limbs break off in storms. In northern climates you also need to consider snow loads.

Most deciduous trees, with their bare limbs in winter months, tend not to alter their shape or accumulate so much snow that they are in danger of breaking. Pines and other evergreens may build up so much snow that the branches sag heavily after major storms and are in greater danger of striking the house or power lines or snapping.

Variety and originality also count for something when selecting trees. Some clients don't mind having the same maples and oaks as all the neighbors have in their yards. However, some clients, especially those who go through the trouble of hiring a professional landscaper, are looking for something a little different, something with a particularly interesting habit and leaf structure. Depending on the situation, you might consider a horse chestnut or larch for such a property, or, for trees set farther away from the house, willows.

Finally, there are some trees that have fallen from favor, either because they are too slow growing or too prone to disease. Many older towns once sported streets lined with elm trees. However, few people are installing elms on their properties these days, for good reason, because of Dutch elm disease.

Trees for Background

Most trees make good background trees, but heavy, dense trees with lush foliage are best suited for this purpose. It is often desirable that background trees be tall enough to show above the house as it is viewed from the front.

Background trees may also be used for screening and buildup. Compact, dense trees make good screens to hide unsightly objects from view. Small trees may be used with taller trees for background effect. Smaller trees can provide gradual buildup in foliage mass by serving as an intermediary planting between shrubs and larger trees.

Specimen Trees

Plants that are outstanding due to form, foliage, flowers, fruit, or other characteristics are known as specimen plants. The special characteristic of the specimen plant may be seasonal, such as trees that flower in the spring. Specimen plants should provide a point of interest, but should always be an integral part of the overall plan and should never call attention to themselves at the expense of the general picture.

Almost any tree that is not also being used as a street or background tree can serve as a specimen tree. For example, if there are no birches on the property or nearby, a circular cluster of white birches growing very close together in the front yard may be quite striking. Species of trees with red leaves, particularly large leaves, thorns, or berries, can also make interesting specimen trees.

Street Trees

Street trees are always trees with high branches that will not obstruct the view of traffic. They should also be chosen for their neat appearance and long life. This will reduce maintenance and replacement of the trees. In some urban locations where smog and other pollutants are common, you should also consider the trees' ability to thrive under these conditions.

The selection of street trees involves considering many limiting factors. The primary limitation is usually space available. Most street trees may be positioned under overhead utility wires. There may be size limits due to the need for road visibility. Because of these many limitations, much study and care should go into the selection of

street trees. You may find that lists of compact growing trees will provide many possibilities.

Be aware that in many municipalities the city actually owns a strip of property starting at the edge of the pavement and running several feet into the front yard. Any trees growing in this space belong to the city, and you cannot cut them down (or in some cases plant new ones) without a permit.

Fruit Trees

Do not overlook the use of fruit trees in landscape design. Fruit trees serve a dual purpose, as part of a design and as a source for fruit, to the delight of most clients. Apples, cherries, peaches, and many other fruit trees may give very satisfactory results in planting plans. Dwarf varieties give you many size options for fruit trees, but you must be aware of pollination requirements if the clients want fruit. Some trees must have more than one variety of fruit tree for pollination, while others are self-pollinating.

Fruit trees intended to produce edible fruit generally require more work than many homeowners realize. Find out how serious the homeowner is about harvesting fruit (for one thing, it may take several years and considerable pruning and maintenance to reach the fruit-bearing stage). If the desire is more aesthetic than productive, species like crab apples often do better and are more attractive than edible-apple trees.

Shrubs

The wide variety of shrubs available to the landscape designer is both a blessing and a challenge. With so many shrubs to choose from, it can be confusing and at times overwhelming. Shrubs, like trees, should perform a function. The type of planting bed you are designing will determine the function of the shrubs you are selecting. The basic types of planting beds are:

- **Foundation Plantings**
- **Entrance Designs**
- **Shrub Borders**
- **Accent Plantings**

Once again we will briefly discuss each type.

Foundation Plantings

Foundation plantings are usually shrubs and are traditionally used to cover the exposed and sometimes ugly foundations of houses. For newer houses, which often do not have exposed foundations to cover up, the foundation plantings form a transition between the house and the front yard. Shrubs in a foundation planting soften the hard corners of the house and relieve the visual monotony of the house's straight lines.

The entrance planting is part of the foundation planting. The main entrance door is the center of interest in the house design and the foundation planting. The entrance development should work into the foundation planting. As with any planting around the house, the foundation planting should show off and complement the house. Therefore, the foundation planting design depends on the individual house.

Most houses make too abrupt a contact with the ground surrounding them. To give a pleasing effect, this feeling of abruptness must be broken. A few carefully placed plants will serve this purpose.

In many situations, the landscape designer uses plantings at the corners of the building. In general, the tallest shrubs of the foundation plants are placed at the corners of the home to soften the architectural lines. Another place where taller plants are used is in any angles formed by the building. Surrounding these plants with shrubs that are gradually less tall creates an eye-pleasing transition. These shorter shrubs cover up the bottom of the larger plants. They also help by giving a more attractive mass of foliage that blends nicely into the lawn area. Lower or medium shrubs are placed under windows and along the sides of the house.

The general form of the foundation planting of shrubs is dish shaped. Of course, some plants rise above or drop below this general line. Be concerned with the general shape instead of details. This same dish shape is more or less typical of shrub elevations along the other three sides of the house; that is, large shrubs at the corners of buildings, with lower shrub groupings along the sides.

Conifer shrubs are commonly used in foundation plantings. This is particularly true in colder regions where conifers provide winter color. Many low-growing conifers, such as junipers and dwarf pines, can be used effectively in foundation plantings. However, very rarely does an entire planting of low growing conifers show off a house to its best advantage.

A combination of deciduous and coniferous plant material almost always gives the best effects. It is also a good idea to repeat conifer shrubs in shrub borders and other plantings away from the house. This produces a much better winter effect than if they are all concentrated immediately adjacent to the house.

There is a tendency to use conifer trees in foundation plantings. This is a poor use for conifer trees, since they can grow to heights of up to 80 feet. In general, these trees cannot be pruned satisfactorily to retain a low form for more than a few years. Their size is then too large for the size of the house. In other words, they are not in scale with the house. Those conifer trees that will withstand shearing finally assume stiff, formal shapes.

Upright, pyramidal trees and shrubs look restless and disturbing when used to a great extent. These flashy foundation plantings often detract from, rather than add to, the beauty and simplicity of the house, so use them sparsely for the most pleasing effect.

There is one other issue to consider in landscape design for the front of a home, and that is security. This is more relevant in some neighborhoods than others. Foundation plants must not provide cover for people who may wish to spy on or break into a home. Nor should any trees close to the house provide access to windows or roofs. One effective solution is to include thorny shrubs into the design in any spot where security might be an issue.

Entrance Design

Although the entrance is part of the foundation planting, it is important enough to discuss separately. The entrance of a home is the public part of the design, and it should be welcoming. A great deal of consideration should be given to the maximum height of shrubs used close to the entrance of the house. This is one of the most common mistakes in shrub selection. You do not want to hide the entrance or have an overgrown look within a few years. Shrubs over 6 feet in height are seldom needed or desired in an entrance design. Overplanting in an entrance planting is also a common problem.

There is also a tendency to use symmetrical plantings (the same on both sides) in an entrance development. Although symmetrical designs are good, do not get in the habit of always matching the shrubs on both sides of the door or walkway. There are other options, such as asymmetrical entrance developments, that are very attractive. They add interest to an entrance development. However, an asymmetrical design must still be balanced. In other words, both sides should have about the same visual "weight." This is a complex subject, but a simple example is that the visual weight of a fat plant on one side can be balanced by two thinner ones of the same height on the opposite side.

The figure on the next page is a good example of the correct use of pyramidal shrubs in an entrance design. This planting is a combination of deciduous and coniferous plant materials. The upright yew to the right of the door repeats the upside-down V shape of the gable in the front of the house, and gives a pleasing accent to the entrance. Notice how skillfully the shrubs and lower-growing juniper have been used to blend these upright plants into the lawn areas. Any number of other plant combinations might have been used in this planting. The trick is to use similarly shaped plants.

Shrub Borders

Shrub borders are informal walls of foliage used in landscaping to define limits. They serve much the same purpose as fences, but create an enclosure border by soft, massed foliage instead of a yard walled by stiff wood or geometric masonry. Shrub borders are used in many parts of a design, such as along property lines, walkways, or driveways. Shrub borders also separate parts of a design, such as the service area from the living garden.

Space is a limiting factor when you consider the use of shrub borders. Shrub borders take much more ground space than fences or walls. On large grounds they may be six or eight plants deep and cover a depth of 20 feet or more. This depth of border is impossible on small home grounds. As a rule, the border on a smaller property is something of a compromise.

First, consider a border where the space is unlimited. Size of plants is still one of the most important considerations. In planning shrub borders, think of the shrubs as belonging to three distinct groups: large, medium, and small. The actual size of shrubs you assign to these

three groupings depends on the size of the area you are planning.

On a large property, the tall shrubs may be 10 to 15 feet tall, the medium shrubs 6 to 10 feet, and the small ones under 5 feet. On a 50 x 150 foot lot the use of such giant shrubs is entirely unsatisfactory. On these smaller grounds, shrubs that will reach a height of 6 to 8 feet are considered large; those 3 to 6 feet tall would be medium; and all those under 3 feet would be classified as small. In most cases, the diameters of these shrubs at maturity will be roughly the same as their height. On even smaller properties, you can select even smaller shrubs and use dwarf shrubs as the small ones.

Along with height, check the spacing of plants in order to choose the correct number of plants for a given area. Shrubs spaced apart at the same distance as their height normally have enough space to develop. For example, shrubs that will grow 6 feet tall should be planted 6 feet apart. This is a good rule of thumb for most shrubs, but remember that some shrubs spread quite wide. Crowding plants is an all-too-common mistake of many landscapers.

The most satisfactory results are generally achieved by grouping plants in a shrub border. Grouping gives a planting unity that is essential for an attractive appearance. The occasional repetition of groups of the same plant is good in a sizable border.

In most small yards 50 feet wide or less, it is difficult to accommodate two borders of a minimum width of 6 to 8 feet. In such cases, a compromise is required. By this we mean the borders can be combined with fences, walls, or hedges to ensure a private area screened from the neighboring yards.

There are several possible solutions:

- A shrub border might be used on one side and a fence on the other. Dwarf shrub varieties will allow you more options along a fenced area.

- Combine flowers and shrubs for satisfactory foliage masses. Shrubs may be used in wider portions, and flowers, vines, or climbing roses in the narrower sections.

- Flower borders may be a possibility, with a fence as a background. Use an occasional shrub to add height, or try vines on the fence. Even a small flowering tree or two will help break up the straight, uninteresting skyline created by most fences.

Shrubs that are used as hedges or other clipped shapes should be thoughtfully chosen. In general, any plant that naturally has a rather compact shape and good foliage may be clipped. Select a plant that will normally grow somewhere near the size of the hedge desired. Also, select the plants with the mature diameter in mind.

Specimen shrubs are similar to specimen trees. They are exceptional because of their form, foliage, flowers, fruit, or some other characteristic. They often help to lift a garden out of the mediocre by adding interest or a striking effect to the border. Specimen shrubs are always an integral part of the overall plan and should never call attention to themselves at the expense of the general picture.

Accent Plantings

A variety of other shrub plantings can be used in a landscape design. Shrubs may be used at the intersections of walks, walks with a driveway, or other areas where different features meet. On small properties, low-growing shrubs should be used in these areas. Give shrubs plenty of space so that they will not overhang the walk or driveway when they are mature.

Island beds are garden beds used in large lawns to break up the area. Small trees and shrubs are the primary features of the island bed. Often five or six shrubs with flower accents are sufficient to create an attractive island bed.

Appearance of the island bed from every angle should be considered. It is important to place the tallest shrubs in the middle of the island and arrange the shorter shrubs around the taller ones. Use the same basic rules that we already covered in placement of shrubs. Be careful not to place the island bed in the middle of the lawn, thus destroying the openness desired in the lawn.

Flowerbeds

A fine flower garden is a creative accomplishment that takes much thought and work. Arranging flowers to make them a part of the garden picture is an art. It may seem overwhelming since there are so many flowers that have different colors, heights, and blooming periods, but some basic principles will help you to organize your ideas and create attractive flowerbeds.

The purpose of this section is to show how flowering plants are organized to become part of the general picture. We will concentrate here on the types of smaller beds that are most often used in combination with other landscaping for small and medium-sized residential lots. Most of these beds are considered borders.

Flower Borders

Flower borders are used in the living garden area in front of shrubbery or along garden walks. They are also used in foundation plantings or in less visible side yards. When planning a flower border, the first consideration is the appropriateness of the location. You must consider the quality of the soil and the amount of sun available. Even more important, consider what part the bed plays in the overall scheme of your design. For example, a flower border that can be seen from the living room or kitchen window will provide more pleasure than one seen only while outdoors.

Consider why a flower border may be appropriate in a particular garden. Is it to add unity to the design? If you have two shrub beds at opposite corners of the backyard, a flower border may be used to connect them, giving the plan unity. Perhaps the design needs more diversity. A flower border in front of shrubs will add color and give contrast to the shrubs. Building up to a point of interest, such as a bench or a garden sculpture, is also a function of a flower border.

Also consider the style of garden being planned. Some people prefer the more traditional flower garden, with flowers that their grandparents grew. Others may prefer a rock garden with alpine plants. Still others prefer a natural garden with wildflowers or other native plants. There are special color gardens, such as blue, yellow, or white gardens, where variations of only one color are used. Although gardens that have flowers blooming throughout the entire growing season are most common and considered best, some people prefer a special season garden, such as one where spring bulbs predominate.

Design Considerations for Flower Borders

Background

Always provide a background against which to display the flower color. Good green foliage is preferred in most cases. It may be a free-growing shrub border or a clipped hedge. In an area with limited space, a vine-covered wire fence or an attractive picket or board fence will be suitable for a background. Consider the color of the fence as part of the design.

Heights of Plants

In general, the taller plants are placed toward the back in a flower border, the medium-growing types in the middle, and the low growers in the front as an edge. Avoid rows of flowers, since this will create a "stair-step" arrangement. Occasionally, taller plants are brought into the middle section and medium-height plants are brought into the foreground to give a more varied effect. However, be careful not to hide shorter plants with taller ones.

In borders that face walks or that are islands, create the background first. Place the taller flowers in the center of the bed, with the remaining plants dropping off in height in all directions.

Width

Naturally, borders can be any width. However, there are certain practical considerations that will influence our designs. To use plants in three general height ranges — tall, medium, and small — a border of 4 to 6 feet wide is necessary. Beyond 6 feet a border becomes unmanageable, since it is difficult to gain access for maintenance.

A border of 3½ feet wide is the minimum for a mixed planting, since you can fit low and medium-sized plants with an occasional tall plant for variety. In borders that are narrower than that, we are limited to row plantings instead of massing plants.

Masses and Individual Plants

The majority of smaller plants should be used in masses of three or more. In a small border, masses of three to seven plants are probably the average. In larger plantings, up to several dozen may be grouped together. Some massing of the larger plants may also be desirable, but this depends on how much space is available.

Repeat the dominant masses throughout the border so that there seems to be an abundance of that special flower in bloom during its blooming season. For instance, clumps of iris scattered at appropriate intervals will bloom more or less at the same time, giving an overall flowering effect to the border. Avoid having masses of the same size. Make some masses larger, some smaller.

Repeat individual plants occasionally, but avoid repetition at equally spaced intervals. Such spacing is monotonous. Individual plants make good specimen plants or accents in a bed.

Forms and Textures

The amazing variety of plant shapes gives you many options when selecting flowers for a border. Many are rounded, some are upright, stiff, and weedy, and others are grasslike. Rounded forms are restful, but can be monotonous when used too frequently. For variety, you need to introduce a few grasslike or upright plants, but not too many.

The texture of flowering plants ranges from feathery, fine foliage to coarse, heavy leaves. Too many dense, compact foliaged plants give a heavy effect. Open, fine plants will add lightness and airiness. Large, plain-leaved plants are used for occasional contrast.

Blooming Periods

Usually the objective of the flower garden is to exhibit continuous blooming. In cold climates, there should be blooming from early spring to late fall. In warmer climates, blooming will occur year-round. Pay close attention to blooming times for flowers in your area to select the right flowers.

Using annuals and perennials together is a good way to increase the blooms in the garden throughout the growing season. Consider the perennials the backbone of the border. Annuals are needed to fill spaces left when perennials stop blooming. Annuals supplement the perennial plantings and can be used as temporary plantings.

Color

Flowers add color to a design, but flower colors should harmonize. Clashing flower colors is not as great a problem as you may think, since the green foliage softens and unifies the effect of the flower colors. There are some bad combinations, of course, and some delightful ones. Here are some aids in planning color combinations.

- Bright and brilliant colors need sunshine to show up best, while softer or pastel colors are more visible in the shade.
- About one-fourth of the color in a border should be darker shades, about one-half in the middle values, and the remaining one-fourth in the lighter tints. This applies to the color of flowers in view at any one time.
- When you think certain colors do not work well together, separate them with light-colored flowers, such as white cream or light yellow.
- Watch the intensity of color. Subdued pastel shades will often look out of place among mostly bright colors. On the other hand, a few brilliant colors may appear spotty in a border composed chiefly of pastel shades.

The amount of knowledge you have about specific plants will help you make decisions on where to use them. You can gain this knowledge by reading technical gardening books and observing various public and private gardens. Take an interest in what you see, and if you don't recognize a species, especially one that impresses you, ask someone about it or look it up in a reference book.

Specialty Gardens

There are many types of specialty gardens that a client may request, or that you may wish to develop for your own property. Some need a good deal of maintenance, such as rock gardens, and others need very little, such as waterwise gardens. All specialty gardens are similar in that they must be a part of the total design plan. Therefore, the specialty garden must harmonize with the general style of the overall design.

Although there are many types of specialty gardens, we will cover five of the most common types: rock gardens, waterwise gardens or xeriscapes, water gardens, native gardens, and container gardens.

Rock Gardens

Rock gardens are gardens that grow alpine plants, small mountain plants, or other small native plants. The rock garden needs maintenance to keep it from becoming a rock museum instead of a garden. However, a properly constructed and planted rock garden is a delight and needs little maintenance.

Keep in mind that a rock garden is for growing plants. The rocks provide a natural environment to display the plants. Rock gardens are usually located on a slope and can be used to replace retaining walls or terrains that are difficult to mow. Often the soil is poor and should be enriched to ensure a successful garden.

A natural setting is usually the best for rock gardens. In such a setting, native rocks will complement the native plants used. When possible, the rock garden should be located in a fairly visible area of the design to take advantage of its unique character.

To establish harmony and naturalness, only one type of rock should be used in a particular garden. Walks and steps within the garden should be made of rocks and materials that blend in naturally with the rest of the design. No matter what type of rocks you use, use rocks large enough to give stability to the garden.

Start the rock garden by removing existing weeds and unwanted vegetation. Then place the larger rocks so that they are partially buried with plenty of soil between the stones. Place each rock so it is anchored firmly and has a solid foundation. Tilt the stones backwards into the soil on a 10- to 30-degree slant and keep the slope fairly constant throughout. Use mulch to retain moisture and keep the weeds from returning.

Low-growing or dwarf shrubs may also be used with flowers, mosses, and bulbs in the rock garden. A background of shrubs and some shade from small, open trees is desirable. One common mistake in planting a rock garden is to treat the rocks merely as containers for the same species of flowers that would be grown in order ordinary flowerbeds and borders. A true rock garden features only plants that grow well among rocks. This means that the forms and textures are quite different from those found elsewhere in the landscape design, which helps give the garden its special interest.

In general, rock garden plants should be low to the ground and somewhat slow growing. They may be strictly foliage plants or have subtle flowers. It is undesirable to hide the rocks themselves or the greenery; lots of showy flowers or plants that grow tall and cover up everything else are counterproductive here.

Waterwise Gardens

Xeriscape is another term for a waterwise (water-conserving) garden. Xeriscapes are used where there is naturally little water. They can save water and maintenance time, and they are ecologically sound.

There are a variety of climates that are arid or semi-arid, and plants must be selected to maximize the local climate.

Is the local area hot and dry, cold and dry, or along the coast? Common sense will tell you that each will require different types of plants. Therefore, the trick to waterwise gardening is to adapt to local conditions.

In areas of heavy development, such as large metropolitan regions, the need for waterwise gardens is especially high. These areas frequently experience periods of drought. During these droughts, irrigation of landscapes may be curtailed. Therefore, planting plans that minimize the dependence upon irrigation are particularly sensible.

A waterwise garden is more than just a few cacti planted in a bed of decorative stones. You can use a wide variety of trees, shrubs, grasses, annual and perennial flowers, and bulbs. Native plants are often used in xeriscapes, although nonnative plants are certainly acceptable, if they are adaptable to the local conditions. Sand or decorative stones may be used as mulch and as part of the design. Whatever material is used, remember that mulches are important to help retain as much moisture as possible.

Water Gardens

Water features are very common in gardens, but not all water features are water gardens. Water gardens are usually composed of a pond or pool with a variety of plants growing in, near, and around the water. Therefore, you must select plants that will grow in the water (usually in containers), at the water edge, and around the pond or pool, where it is drier.

The sizes of water gardens vary greatly. Some are quite small and fit even in a patio garden. Others may be pools that are part of large, formal gardens. The two basic types of water gardens are the natural pond and the ornamental pool.

The natural pond is best located in a quiet corner of the design. Native plants are often used, although this is not a requirement. Rocks or stones are often used at the water's edge for natural transition. Fish, frogs, or other animals are great additions to the natural pond.

The ornamental pool is usually more centrally located in the design than the natural pool. Often, it is the center of attraction and is located close to the house or patio. There are many styles of ornamental pools, and they can fit into a wide variety of landscape designs. Goldfish are the most common animal in the ornamental pool.

A balanced selection of plants will keep the pool or pond healthy. Plants are essential to maintain oxygen levels needed to support the animals and to keep excessive algae from growing. Therefore, carefully select plants that will not only grow well in your water garden, but keep it healthy.

Native Gardens

Native gardens take advantage of the plants that grow locally, and do not include nonnative plants. Meadow or wildflower gardens are common types, but any region will have a wide variety of native plants to create a garden.

Native gardens are low maintenance but they should not be neglected altogether. Wildflowers must be reseeded and relocated to keep the look you want. The trick to native gardens is to make them look as though they are more natural than they really are.

A common objective for the native garden is to attract wildlife. Plants must be used to provide food and shelter for wildlife, even if you supplement these with food and housing. Water must also be provided. Study the animals and plants in your area. The more you know about the region, the more likely it is you will be able to design a successful native garden. However, be aware of any local laws that may prohibit the feeding of wild animals in some localities. Also, consider the well-being of the animals at a particular site, and be sure they will not face predators or have to cross a road or enter a type of neighborhood that will put them in danger.

Container Gardens

Plants in containers add accents to a design, or may be the total design. Container plants can transform a patio or terrace into a complete garden. There are so many sizes and shapes of containers, and of plants that will grow in them, that a wide variety of designs is possible.

Plants in containers may be placed on tables or on the ground. They can hang from walls or ceilings. Dwarf trees, as well as shrubs, can be grown in containers. Plants can grow tall, climb up attractive supports, or hang down from above. A cherry tomato basket or a kitchen herb garden gives food as well as viewing pleasure.

Although container gardening is flexible and provides wonderful additions to many designs, you must be aware of some problem areas. Sufficient drainage is needed in all containers. If the container is not built to supply drainage, then an ample layer of stone must be added to the bottom of the container to keep the plant roots from lying in water.

Of course, sufficient water must be supplied to the plants. Do not assume that just because plants are outside they will receive enough water naturally. Soil in most small containers and hanging baskets has a tendency to dry out much more rapidly than soil in the surrounding ground, and it also has a greater tendency to overheat on hot days.

Watering very large plants may be very time consuming. There are many devices that will save time, such as self-watering containers. Polymer crystal or granules that you mix with potting soil will hold water and slowly release it to reduce the need to water frequently. Mulches are also very helpful.

Pruning and "deadheading" are needed to keep plants at the appropriate size and shape and to increase flowering. Deadheading means removing blossoms once they are dried up but before they have gone to seed, to encourage the plant to produce more of them. Many container plants must be staked or supported. In colder climates, winter protection is needed. Roots of container plants can become frozen much more quickly than those planted in the ground.

Selecting Plants for a Vegetable Garden

When planning a vegetable garden, one needs first to determine its main purpose. Some small vegetable gardens, like most flower gardens, are really just for the enjoyment of the gardener. There may be no commercial interest involved, and only a minor thought of raising a significant amount of food for the family. In such a case, the gardener should select species that he or she will enjoy cultivating, that will be aesthetically appealing (as plants, not just as food), and that work well with the limitations of the site and the amount of time and energy the gardener has to devote to the project. Of course, many serious vegetable gardens are intended to be much more productive, and are not just for fun.

With very few exceptions, most vegetables need rich soil and full sunlight to produce at their best. Not all backyard gardens provide this. If the soil is poor you can usually do something

about this, but inadequate sunlight is harder to deal with. On a residential lot the vegetable patch is often not so important that one wishes to cut down all the surrounding trees and structures just to maximize the sun exposure. If a garden gets a lot of sun, but not continuous sun, the gardener may be able to get by with most crops. However, they may take a little longer to mature. This becomes an issue in climates where the growing season is short. If your conditions aren't optimal, you might have to add two or three weeks to the harvest dates cited on the seed packages. Be sure this will not put your crops at risk of being killed by frost before they can be harvested.

One way to compensate for a short growing season, or simply to achieve earlier harvests, is to start vegetables in a greenhouse or a bright and sunny indoor location. Small greenhouses are not as difficult or expensive to install as one might expect, and they can be a real asset to the serious amateur vegetable gardener. Realize, though, that plants started indoors or in a greenhouse may need to be "hardened off" before they can be planted outside. This means they have to become acclimated by being set outdoors, in their pots, for increasingly longer portions of the day before being planted outdoors for good. This is called hardening off because the young plants change physically and develop harder and tougher "skins" on their stems. The leaves will also thicken and often become darker. Transplants that are not hardened off have a lower survival rate. Some may wither or rot, while others may be knocked down by the wind or a heavy downpour.

It is particularly important when planting vegetables to know the needs of the species involved, and to follow the recommended instructions for how warm the soil needs to be before planting. Use a thermometer to measure the soil temperature. Seeds planted too early in the season may

fail to germinate, and even those that do sprout will likely grow more slowly and be less healthy than crops planted in the proper soil conditions.

When selecting your crops, you need to consider not only the nutrient quality of the soil, but the depth of the topsoil and how loose or supple it tends to be. Where the soil is not as deep, or where it has a little too much clay in it and tends to harden a bit each time it dries out, root crops like beets and carrots won't do well. You are better off to plant more-tolerant crops like beans or lettuce in such locations.

If you have bright sun, but for only part of the day, crops like sweet corn will tend to grow too slowly. Corn is an example of a crop that does better in wide-open fields than in most backyard vegetable patches.

One common cause of disappointment that surprises many vegetable growers is problems with pollination. Plants will not produce fruit (and many "vegetables" are actually the fruits of the plants) unless their flowers are pollinated. Wind will spread pollen to a limited degree, but bees are even more effective. If you do not have an adequate number of bees in and around your garden, certain crops that require bee pollination will do poorly even if all other growing conditions are optimized. Bumblebees are very common and effective pollinators, as are many small species of bees and wasps, and a handful of other insects. To some extent the flowers in the vegetable patch will attract bees on their own. Planting flowerbeds near the vegetable patch may also help. However, particularly in urban areas, there may not be enough bees in the general area to perform pollination effectively.

There is currently a crisis in declining bee populations in most parts of North America, and it is causing serious problems not only for backyard gardeners but also for the farming industry. You need to avoid doing anything to make the problem worse, such as overusing insecticide. For certain crops, and particularly in the smaller vegetable patch, you can pollinate vegetable flowers yourself. This works particularly well for plants that have large flowers, such as pumpkins and squash. Learn to identify the male and female flowers and flower parts, and transfer the powdery yellow pollen to the female parts of the flower with delicate strokes of a paintbrush or cotton swab. Doing so can dramatically increase the quantity of vegetables that will develop on these plants. Make sure you use a different brush for each species that you pollinate in this fashion.

Even when bees are abundant, other pollination problems may occur. Bees and wind spread pollen somewhat indiscriminately, and most plants are able to ignore pollen that does not belong to their species. However, when two species are closely related sometimes a plant may use the wrong pollen and thus produce fruits and vegetables of poor quality. It is particularly important not to plant different species of corn, or different members of the squash and pumpkin family, too close together in the garden. This will increase the transfer of the wrong pollen to the wrong flowers.

If you want to avoid a lot of frustration and hassle with your vegetable crop, before planting you should also consider what sorts of pests you will be facing. For example, some backyard gardeners fight a constant battle with slugs. There are various methods, chemical and otherwise, for helping to control them, but if slugs are really abundant at your site, it may be impossible to eradicate them altogether. There are some vegetable seedlings that slugs tend to ravage more than others. They devour string beans and lettuce, for example, but usually leave tomato plants alone (at least until the tomatoes are ripe). Plants like zucchini, cucumbers, and pumpkins are vulnerable to slugs when they first germinate, but soon become coarse and tough, and undesirable to slugs.

Other frequent garden pests include deer, rabbits, gophers, and chipmunks. If these animals are a problem at your site, you may need to design a fence that will keep them out. In the case of deer, this means a fence at least 6, and preferably 8, feet tall. In the case of the burrowing critters it means a fence that extends below the ground line to discourage tunneling. Fences may also add visual appeal, but for the vegetable garden (and some types of flower beds where wild mammals are a problem) aesthetics is not as important as functionality.

In sum, you can save yourself a lot of hassle and disappointment if you plant a vegetable garden for the logistical realities and limitations of the site. There will probably be some crops that just won't do well for you. It is best to pass these up and stick with something that is easier and more gratifying. There is something satisfying about a bumper crop, whatever that crop may be.

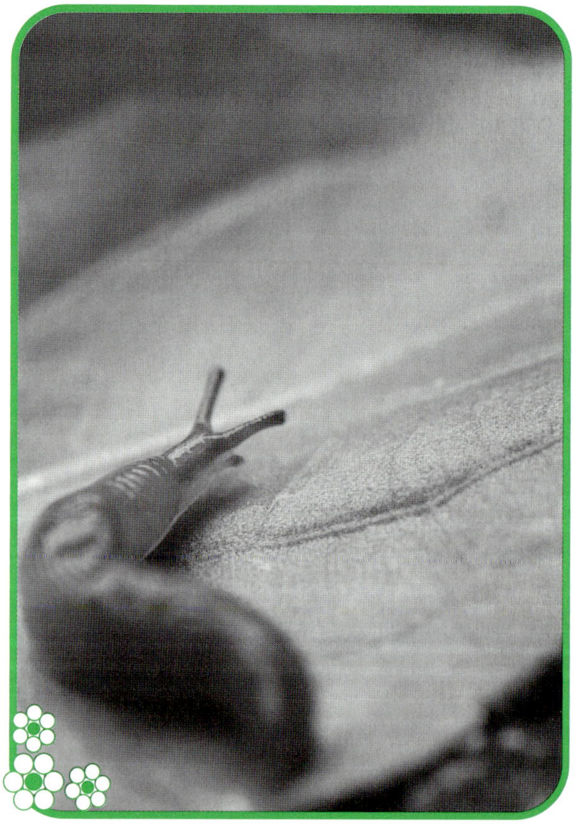

Gardening Tip

Here's a highly effective tip for protecting vegetable or flower seedlings and transplants from persistent slugs. Throughout the year, wash out and save any empty large plastic food containers you acquire. Discard the tops and cut out the bottoms. Ideally the containers should be at least 6 inches in diameter. Now get a 2-inch-wide roll of transparent packing tape. Cut about ten 4-inch strips and temporarily hang them by their edges so they don't stick to themselves or one another. You will use these to create a wide horizontal "flange" around the top edges of each container. Lay each strip horizontally across the top edge of the container such that most of the strip is outside the container. Let the end of one strip just touch the end of the next one so the strips connect to one another. Then make a few cuts in the portion of the tape that lies over the inside of the container and bend the pieces downward to stick them to the inside walls. There should now be a collar of tape outside the rim and parallel to the base, with the sticky side facing down.

Now attach additional strips to the underside of your collar with their sticky sides upward, making a second layer of tape. The two layers are sticky side to sticky side, so the finished collar is no longer sticky on either surface.

Take your barriers out to the garden and push them down slightly into loosened soil to prevent anything from crawling under the barrier or the wind from blowing it away. Plant your seeds or transplants within the protective "castle." For added protection, once you are finished you can lightly smear vapor rub jelly on both sides of the tape collar. The camphor in the vapor rub will help discourage any slugs ambitious enough to try to crawl along the underside of the flange and up over the top.

These slug barriers will work for only a few weeks. Eventually the camphor wears off, rain will splash mud on the collars, and a few persistent slugs will be able to get around them. However, by that time your transplants should be tall and sturdy enough to survive, and you can then cut through and remove the collars.

Since this technique is a bit labor intensive, it is more suited to a backyard vegetable patch than a whole field of vegetables. However, because slugs and other pests often have more hiding and breeding places in backyard gardens than in open fields, it can be well worth the effort.

The Ten Most Common Mistakes Made by Gardeners and Landscapers

This concluding chapter focuses on common mistakes in gardening and landscaping and how to prevent or correct them. Learning how to avoid or overcome these problems will make you more knowledgeable than the average home gardener. In fact, professional gardeners and landscapers are hired because they apply their expertise and skills to yield superior results. They are expected to avoid the pitfalls of inexperienced gardeners.

Some mistakes happen because the wrong type of care is administered to a particular species of plant, but these can largely be avoided by consulting technical manuals for procedural details. However, there are some types of more significant or at least more pervasive mistakes that often surprise gardeners. In the following paragraphs we will identify several of these and their root causes, and explain how to correct and avoid these particular problems.

Failure to Match Plants to the Site's Conditions

People are naturally attracted to some plants more than to others. When some people first acquire a new property with the chance to design and plant their own garden for the first time, often they see it as a chance to surround themselves with flowers, shrubs, and trees that interest and excite them the most. They start buying simply those plants that look attractive, and they become determined that one way or another these items will work.

There are two serious problems with this approach. First of all, impulse purchases tend to take gardeners outside of any cohesive overall plan for the garden. Individually the plants may be interesting, but when thrown together on a whim they simply don't fit together.

The second and bigger problem is it disregards the laws of nature and botany. Nature is neither forgiving nor accommodating. It doesn't work with you; you need to work with it. Some plants, however appealing they may be, have little or no chance of thriving, or perhaps even of surviving, at a given site. It is for this reason that gardeners must be certain that the soil, moisture, sunlight, and climate conditions of a site will be suitable for whatever plants are intended.

Before any sort of plan can be formulated, let alone any specific plants selected, the professional garden designer needs to study the site and find out, in considerable detail, its physical and chemical qualities. Minor adjustments in things like acidity or alkalinity of soil can be attempted, but if the site isn't already pretty close to suitable for a particular plant, chances are you can't make it so, and it would be a waste of time and money to attempt to do so.

This is why professional gardeners need to have an understanding of a soil that goes beyond the quick conclusions of many amateurs. Most gardeners know to check pH (acidity or alkalinity), but cohesiveness, drainage, aeration, and the presence or absence of key nutrients are just as important. Nitrogen and phosphorus are necessary, but for many plants the most essential element is the right amount of water, and soils of certain textures can make achieving a specific water content all but impossible. Soil chemistry and topography (the lay of the land as it affects drainage) determine how well a site will hold or shed water. Irrigation can make a difference, but not if the soil won't work with the water you try to provide.

Light and climate are also extremely important to the long-term success of any plant. What people sometimes forget, however, is that the amount of sunlight an empty plot of land receives isn't the same thing as the amount of sunlight specific portions of a garden will

receive once all the plants and structures are installed and developed. Many plants struggle to survive when they grow in the shade of a much larger plant. Gardeners should always remember that plants grown in close quarters will compete for resources. A site may have optimal conditions before anything is planted, but if plants are grown too close to each other, some might not get the light and water they need. Therefore, before planting or purchasing anything for a garden, it is essential to think about each plant's unique growing needs and whether they can be met in the site as it is planned.

Improper Watering

If it weren't for our ability to water or irrigate our gardens and fields, three-quarters of the species we plant would fail to survive. A relatively limited number of species of flowering plants, shrubs, and trees grow naturally in any given location. Nature has many methods for distributing seeds and pollen widely and somewhat randomly, but only a handful of types survive, sprout, and do well at particular locations. One reason others fail to survive is that they are squeezed out physically by more aggressive species. The other main reason, apart from soil chemistry, is that they cannot withstand the droughts or the temperature shifts that a particular site experiences during at least part of the season. Therefore, they need us to provide them with water so they aren't completely at the mercy of the weather. Providing water to a lawn or garden is a much more complicated task than first meets the eye. Here is a brief listing of some of the reasons why.

- Water must penetrate the soil all the way down to the lowest level of a plant's roots. If only the upper portion of the soil gets wet, eventually the lower roots will die off and the plants will try to survive by expanding their shallow, surface roots. This can lead to several problems that will cause the plant to fail. The depth to which gardens or shrubbery should be watered varies by species, so it can be tricky to control how much water each plant gets. In general, lawns should be watered until the water has penetrated to a depth of 4 to 6 inches. Do not water excessively to the point where puddles of standing water form on the surface.

- After being watered, the soil needs to dry out somewhat before it should be watered again. Why? Mainly because soil that is constantly wet will begin to bloom with harmful microorganisms such as bacteria and fungi, and larger creatures such as slugs can then attack the plants and cause a variety of diseases.

- A soil's ability to drink up water changes over time. Water may penetrate a loose soil well at first. However, over time the soil may become compacted, and less water gets below the surface. Also, some soils that contain a lot of clay tend to seal themselves off by forming a hard crust when they dry, stopping surface water from getting through.

- Over the long term, water supplied through irrigation will change, and quite possibly harm, the soil's chemistry. Why? Because unlike rainwater, which is virtually pure, water used in irrigation contains a significant quantity of dissolved minerals, including a small but potentially damaging amount of dissolved salts. Decades of irrigation of some farming areas gradually increase the mineral level and salt content in soils and can make them no longer suitable for growing certain crops.

- You water a garden mainly to get water into the soil where the plant's roots lie. However, at the same time you inevitably get water on the plants. If the plants stay wet for too long, mold and other diseases may start. Also, for certain species of plants droplets of water on leaves can act like tiny magnifying glasses to allow sunlight to burn spots in leaves, and the damaged areas become a starting point for other types of diseases and problems. This problem is often overstated in gardening folklore, but it can happen to some types of delicate plants. On the other hand, some plants absorb more water through their leaves than through their roots, and they benefit from being watered or misted often. Also, particularly for young transplants on very hot days, watering the leaves will help cool them as the water evaporates. Thus, in some situations watering plants in the midday sun is a good idea, and in other situations it is a bad idea. This is why gardening manuals are so complicated, and why you need to look up the requirements and preferences of individual species you are working with.

- The size of individual water droplets affects how well they will be absorbed by the ground, or how quickly they may begin to merge into rivulets and run off. An intense yet short watering with large, heavy drops does not penetrate the soil as effectively as a slow, gentle soaking. This is why thundershowers can be all but useless in alleviating drought conditions. Most of the water runs off the surface, and no matter how much water may have fallen during a few minutes of heavy downpour, the next day the ground may be as dry as it

was before the storm passed. Also, heavy downpours compact soil, whereas a gentle rain will actually help loosen it.

- In most cases the best time to water is early in the morning. Watering in the evening or at night is not recommended for most lawns and gardens because it encourages the growth of fungi. Watering at midday is inefficient because much of the water evaporates before it can be absorbed.

Once again, the professional gardener needs to learn from nature. As you read more about gardening, pay close attention to watering instructions. They are often very specific, and there's a reason for this.

Improper Lawn Mowing

Lawns are an important part of the landscaping of almost all residential and institutional sites. It can be very difficult to establish a high-quality lawn at some sites, and maintaining a healthy lawn can be even more challenging.

Few plants in nature other than grasses can survive having their heads chopped off on a regular basis. Many species of grass not only survive but thrive as a result of mowing. However, this doesn't change the fact that a freshly mowed lawn is in fact a damaged lawn in need of healing. Until the individual grass plants are able to heal, they are at risk of dehydrating. The passage of the lawn mowers and the workers operating them compacts the soil, and this problem may worsen over time. Also, the severed portion of the grass blades must be either removed from the lawn or else reduced to small pieces by a mulching mower so they will dry out and decompose quickly without harming the living plants.

Dehydration is perhaps the most important concern. The ability of grass not to wither after mowing depends on the temperature and humidity at the time the lawn is cut, and on how much of the blade is cut (the height to which the grass is mowed). As you progress from the tip of a blade of grass toward the root, the stalk becomes wider and so do the vessels that carry fluids. The wider they are, the longer it will take them to seal off after a cut, and the more fluid the plant will lose.

All types of grass have an ideal mowing height, and it is very important that they not be cut shorter than this. The amount cut at any one mowing is equally important. In general you should not cut more than the top third of the grass blades. If you wait too long between mowings, you might find you are cutting half the blade or more. This is why it is impossible to state how often a lawn should be mowed, because the growth rate is dramatically faster early in the season and slows during dry spells. The lawn should be mowed when allowing it to continue growing would necessitate the removal of more than one-third of the blade height. That could be once every two or three days, or two or three weeks, depending on growing conditions.

Mowing height is also affected by lawn usage. Some high-quality ornamental lawns can be cut as short as half an inch, but this is not the norm. For lawns that are used for walking or playing, a height of 2 to 3 inches is recommended, with greater height in shaded areas. It is not necessary to mow all parts of a property to one standard height. Rather, vary the height in specific areas depending on conditions and usage.

Temperature and humidity are also very important factors. It is best that lawns not be mowed in the full heat of midday, especially during periods of hot, dry weather, because water loss from the cut blades will be accelerated. Some people think that they can make up for cutting at the wrong time of day by watering the lawn immediately afterwards, but this doesn't always work well. Also, if the water doesn't penetrate to the roots, and sometimes even if it does, the natural processes by which plants take it up require some time, and dehydration may outrun rehydration.

People often mow their lawns somewhat out of habit. The timing will be based on their own convenience, rather than the needs of the lawn and the actual conditions. People continue to mow their lawns during droughts, and they often mow at the wrong time of day. If they don't like mowing, they may cut the grass shorter than the recommended height to try to delay the next mowing. All of these are bad practices.

Unfortunately, lawn maintenance companies and hired grounds crews often make the same mistakes, but for a different reason. They tend to work according to schedules, and sometimes they let the demands of the schedule and of running the business take precedence over the changing needs of the lawns they are supposed to be maintaining. Sometimes the motivation is simply a financial one. Realities on the ground may dictate that mowing be suspended during a drought, but the staff won't get paid if they don't mow, so they mow it anyway. Also, time-of-day issues and weather conditions may be overlooked because there is a need to keep workers busy all day long, and it may seem like too much trouble to schedule other tasks during the times when mowing is not recommended.

Other damaging problems can arise during periods of prolonged rain, drizzle, or cold. It is not a good idea to mow a lawn that is saturated with water. The blades tend not to work as efficiently. The cuttings don't behave as they should and may not become properly mulched, even if a mulching mower is used. The soil is soft, so mowers and footsteps may damage it

and the underlying root systems in the lawn. Also, although dehydration may not be a factor, a blooming of microorganisms may be. Those mushrooms that you see growing on lawns after a prolonged rainy spell are a more visible example of the many types of organisms that multiply rapidly in moist conditions. Most of these bacteria and fungi are too small to see but can be very destructive, especially to lawns that are weakened from a mowing.

Failure to Establish a Pleasing Overall Design

In order for a garden to be visually pleasing, it must first be well designed. Proper design involves such considerations as a garden's location, boundaries, and intended use. It also applies aesthetic principles such as balance, symmetry, texture, and complementary colors.

Garden design should occur before any plants, structures, and features are purchased. Unfortunately, too many amateur gardeners neglect this all-important step. Even if they choose attractive plants and architecture that suit the site, the end result is likely to appear unappealing and disorganized if they do not install these items according to a layout that was carefully planned from the very beginning.

Design is hard to learn in some ways because it involves several different elements that must exist simultaneously, and a change in any one of them may affect more than one of the other variables. You can't learn design simply by memorizing a list of rules or steps. You must truly understand what is going on.

Amateur gardeners often don't understand this. They pick plants they like, or they pick plants that they think look good together when they are first installed, without considering how they will change over time as they grow. Many gardeners overcrowd their beds. They have only so much space to work with, and they think they are making the most of it, failing to realize that more is not necessarily better. Some people make this mistake in interior decorating, overcrowding rooms and juxtaposing things that clash and create a sense of clutter. Gardeners

tend to make the same mistake, except here it can become worse, because their additions expand and make the space even more crowded.

One of the most important ways in which professional gardeners or landscapers distinguish themselves from amateurs is by mastering the principles and the practices of successful landscape and garden design. This expertise is a significant reason why these professionals are valued and sought.

Failure to Develop a Garden for Year-round Interest

This is a very common problem, perhaps because this element is so easy to overlook. Items in a garden not only keep growing, but they keep changing. Too many amateur-designed gardens look really attractive for only a few weeks of the year, if even that. The rest of the time they look like a work in progress. The owner of the garden is waiting for it to become attractive, rather than enjoying its attractions.

There are many ways this can happen, but they all center around failing to plan ahead, and failing to be familiar enough with each plant species to know how it will change over time. To give one very small but common example, many amateur gardeners want a garden that quickly becomes filled with blossoms in the early spring. So, they plant large beds or sections of crocuses, daffodils, or tulips. All of these plants are beautiful, but their blossoms last only a few weeks. When the blooms fade the garden starts to look like fall is approaching, rather than summer. The frustrated gardener thinks about inserting some annual transplants, but is afraid to dig up the soil for fear of damaging and killing the bulbs.

Some people go to the opposite extreme on this. They limit themselves only to species of flowers that tend to bloom repeatedly or continuously throughout the growing season. This way their beds always have flowers in them. That's probably better than a bed that becomes nothing but dying stalks after a time, but it also creates a garden that is static and monotonous.

Professional gardeners have a better approach. They ensure that there is something in bloom throughout the season, but not necessarily the same things throughout. They plan for one type of plant to blossom once another has begun to wither. As they lay out the beds, they can envision what the garden will look like at each phase of the season. Good gardeners make sure that species that die off don't get in the way of the new blooms. They make sure there is a balance in how the plants that are in bloom at any given time are distributed throughout the bed or beds. They make sure that plants in the foreground don't block or overshadow those behind them. All of this is really just an extension of garden design, but with more emphasis on seasonality.

Crowding

Too many flowerbeds and landscape elements established by amateurs start out, or become over time, seriously overcrowded. Not only is this aesthetically unappealing, but it eventually causes weakness and disease among the crowded plants. It becomes difficult and tedious to maintain beds because of all the dead growth and weeds that need to be removed. Before you know it, local plants sprout and the garden is a meadow. Actually, it becomes worse than a meadow, because when many of the delicate species get stressed by crowding, it may become a dying meadow.

As with many other gardening problems, the key to avoiding this is to know the plants you are using and to plan ahead for growth and allow space for it in the installation. However, this is not quite so simple. You cannot create a garden that looks half empty just because eventually, in the long term, it will fill out. Often, depending on how quickly a given plant will grow and fill out, it is beneficial to place "temporary" plants, or plants that will grow quickly but then die back quickly, into spaces that will eventually be filled by their surrounding elements.

This principle applies not only to planting shrubbery that will gradually get larger over several seasons. It can even be applicable to a bed of annuals, and the vegetable garden is the perfect example. Many gardeners have limited space for vegetable crops, and they want to get the highest yield possible from it. Some plants, such as cucumbers and pumpkins, gradually become large and need a lot of space. However, early in the growing season they aren't using all the space they will eventually occupy. This creates an opportunity to plant some quick-developing, short-season crops such as lettuce, radishes, or string beans in the meantime.

Another example of using space well in the vegetable garden involves coordinating ground-level plants with plants that grow high on tall stalks. Similarly, plants that need full sunlight can be grown near others that do rather well in some degree of shade. The classic example of this is planting corn and pumpkins together. Corn needs bright full sun, which it gets because of its tall stalks, even if other plants are growing at lower elevations. Pumpkins also like sun, but they don't seem to mind if it is mottled by the shadows cast by corn stalks. You get two successful crops, both of which need considerable room to grow, in the same space.

Failure to Prune and Maintain Trees and Shrubs

This is a subtle problem but it is very pervasive. It springs from the mistaken belief that once you plant a tree and it survives its first couple of seasons it takes care of itself for the rest of its life.

One day go for a walk in the woods and take a few minutes to look carefully at some of the trees you find. You will find many that are dead or dying, or that have broken or dead limbs, or whose leaves are afflicted with fungal or viral diseases or insects, or that have rotting portions or portions infested with carpenter ants, or that have lost most of their lower limbs and seem to be hanging on to life by a handful of upper branches. All of this is perfectly natural, of course. It is the rare tree indeed that lives to old age and spreads out to assume its full potential shape and habit.

In our yards and gardens, however, we aim for a much higher success rate for individual trees that we plant. To achieve it requires professional knowledge and care. Pruning is not only for appearances. It is also done to remove material that may become diseased and to make a tree more stable and less vulnerable to damage.

The long-term health of trees is also affected by the quality and depth of the soil in which they grow, by the trees surrounding them, and by the amount of moisture that is able to penetrate to their roots, which depends not only on rainfall but on the degree of compaction of the soil. A tree not planted under ideal circumstances may do okay for a time but then fail.

Also, certain species in certain areas are highly susceptible to diseases and pests, and a tree that appears to be doing well can quickly (or in some cases slowly) succumb to blight. For all of these reasons and more, professional gardeners and landscapers need to know much more about trees and shrubs than the average homeowner in order to provide quality installation and maintenance of these important plants, which are among the keys to the success of almost any landscape design.

Incorrect Use of Fertilizers and Pesticides

Many inexperienced people seem to assume that a quick reading of a label or chat with a sales clerk will qualify them to administer chemicals that are capable of causing harm not only to plants, but to the people and animals who come in contact with these substances, and to the environment as a whole. That skull and crossbones you see on many of these products is there for a reason.

Some people understand this about pesticides (which are, after all, essentially poisons) but fail to be as cautious when it comes to fertilizers. Many people think of fertilizer as a form of food, and this gives it a very benign image. However, fertilizer is a highly concentrated type of food. Too much of it can be dangerous.

One common problem with fertilizer is that it is sometimes hard to get it to the roots, which are the only parts that can use it, without getting it on the leaves and stalks, unless the fertilizer is applied before planting. Roots will absorb fertilizer chemicals very slowly, and in highly diluted form. The leaves, which are far more delicate, cannot withstand the harshness of many of these concentrated chemicals. This is why it is always best, whenever possible, to get fertilizer and nutrients into the soil before you plant. Once again, this requires planning. You need to add ingredients that will release nutrients right away, but that will also continue to do so over an extended period of time.

Fertilizer is no cure for poor soil conditions, or soil that is inappropriate for the type of plant being grown. Pesticides are sometimes necessary but they come with many risks and side effects. These days, in part because of growing environmental awareness, there is a desire on the part of many to limit the use of pesticides and fertilizers, and to find natural alternatives to them. These alternatives can be truly effective in some cases, and it benefits today's professional gardener and landscaper to be knowledgeable about these options.

The more important point to make is, as they say in medicine, an ounce of prevention is worth a pound of cure. With forward-looking design and planting methods, many of the problems that cause people to scramble for chemical solutions can be avoided in the first place. Some plants are hardier than others in any given situation. Some plants are more resistant to diseases or pests than others. All other factors being equal, selecting the plant with the stronger chance for success heads off a lot of plant-medicine issues before they ever arise.

Failure to Provide Proper Drainage

Too much water is as devastating for plants as too little. It encourages the grown of microorganisms that can cause disease. More importantly it inhibits air from reaching the soil. People often underestimate the importance of gases in the soil to the metabolism of plants.

Most drainage problems are caused by topography: the way the ground slopes, causing water on the surface either to run off it or collect on it. In the design of any property that is about to be developed, topography is the first and perhaps most important issue. It starts with the architect who designs the house and, just as importantly, decides where on the lot to place it. Ideally all properties should be designed so the house or building is on a high point and the ground slopes away from it in all directions. In practice this may be difficult or impossible to achieve on certain lots. However, building a house on a high point is usually worth the trouble because it greatly reduces the risk of leaks and flooding.

If it is not possible to situate a building so the ground slopes away from it, it is often possible to modify the contours of the surface around the house to help direct at least some of the water away from the building. This is commonly done through the use of either drainage trenches or embankments. However, this won't always be adequate protection where water flows readily under the surface and may collect around the base of the foundation. In northern climates the situation may become far worse in the winter because the frozen ground may act like a giant slide, propelling melting snow or winter rain toward the building in overwhelming quantities.

Water that puddles up in part of the yard is a less serious problem than water that puddles up around the house, but it can still lead to problems that diminish the value of the property. Also, even when water can be diverted away, care must be taken to ensure that this does not lead to erosion and loss of soil, or the formation of unsightly gullies. Proper vegetation

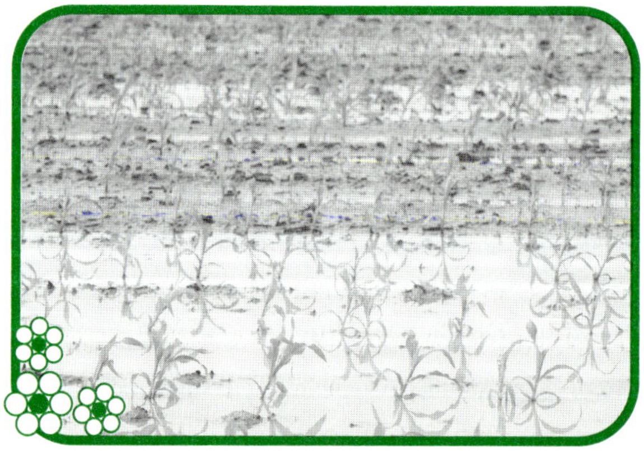

can play a key role in preventing erosion. However, in places that are steeper or are exposed to a lot of water, it may be necessary to add rocks to the site, or build a series of reinforced stone walls and terraces (flat areas adjacent to the walls), in order to keep the soil where it belongs. Even when a wall is constructed of stone or concrete, drainage is still an issue, because the weight of backed-up water may crack a retaining wall. Retaining walls are intended to hold back soil, not water. Often pipes that go through the wall are installed during the wall's construction to allow any water that collects behind the wall to flow through to the other side.

Landscaping is also important in disguising certain types of changes made for the sake of drainage. A good design conceals the fact that certain features have been added because of a drainage issue. These features must be incorporated into a pleasing and balanced overall design for the property.

Losing the War against Weeds

By definition, weeds are unwanted plants that sprout up in gardens or lawns. In most cases they are native wild plants. Fifty years ago, weeding a garden and manually removing weeds from lawns were by far the most labor-intensive aspects of gardening and property maintenance. Then two innovations reduced the volume of effort needed in this regard. The first was herbicides (chemicals that kill plants) that were designed to target only weeds. The second was the development of some mulches, consisting of inert materials such as woodchips or crushed walnut shells, that cover the soil around desirably mature plants, making it harder for weeds to sprout up because of reduced access to sunlight at the ground surface. In certain types of gardens mulching is also done with fabric.

Both strategies are still in use today. However, the use of herbicides is rapidly falling from favor because of environmental concerns. The chemicals often kill more than just weeds, and they end up seeping into the groundwater. Mulching is a more benign activity, and therefore a highly recommended one, but it is not practical in all situations. Mulching works only when the plants you want are already mature enough to have risen well above the layer of mulch, and the weeds have not yet started. Besides blocking weeds, mulches can play a valuable role in holding more moisture in the soil. However, mulch is less practical in some vegetable gardens or in beds that are more or less covered with flowers or small flowering plants. Obviously, mulches are also of no use in stopping weeds from growing in lawns.

There are many other strategies for combating weeds, and these will be covered in more-technical gardening books. One of the simplest is proper lawn maintenance, since healthy lawns are naturally more resistant to weeds.

Even with all of the strategies for inhibiting or reducing weeds, weeding will still be necessary in many types of gardens. The design of the beds will have a lot to do with how simple or practical weeding may be. Any garden or bed must be designed with a weed control strategy in mind before planting. If you create a bed that will be vulnerable to weeds, or that will be difficult to access for efficient weed removal, you increase the likelihood that the battle will be lost sooner or later. Also, excessive tilling or cultivating of the soil once plants have sprouted can damage some plant roots and cause other problems.

When weeding becomes necessary, as in certain types of vegetable plantings, correct weeding technique is essential. This requires knowledge of individual plants and their requirements. Some plants, such as tomatoes, tend to have shallow roots that are easily damaged if the ground around the stalk is deeply disturbed with an implement such as a garden hoe. Some plants cannot withstand such disturbances, whereas others, such as string beans, actually benefit from having soil vigorously loosened and pulled toward the stalks from both sides of the row. In some cases you are better off using the blade of the hoe to simply cut the weed close to the surface rather than disturb the underlying layers, even though this means the weeds will eventually regrow. In other cases it is better to completely uproot the weeds with deeper strokes of the hoe. In still other situations, sometimes all that is needed is to pull loose soil up over the weeds to smother them, without cutting or uprooting them.

Like many gardening topics, weeding involves a few general principles that are relatively easy to learn, as well as many details that require specialized knowledge. The good news is that you do not need to memorize tons of technical information to be an effective gardener or landscaper. You can always consult reference materials when you are faced with a particular project or problem. As you read more about this subject and gain more practical experience, your expanding knowledge of plants and procedures will enable you to become a true professional in gardening and landscaping.

A Glimpse at Some of the World's Greatest Gardens

Garden of Versailles, France

Jardin du Luxembourg, Paris, France

Garden of Monplaisir Palace, St. Petersburg, Russia

Tivoli Gardens, Copenhagen, Denmark

Taj Mahal, Agra, India

Ho Chi Minh Mausoleum, Hanoi, Vietnam

Garden and Chateau Langeais, Loire Valley, France

Kew Gardens, London, England

Keukenhof Gardens, Lisse, the Netherlands

Emirates Palace Hotel, Abu Dhabi, UAE

Notre Dame Cathedral Park, Paris, France

Garden of Peterhof, St. Petersburg, Russia

Queen Elizabeth Park, Vancouver, British Columbia, Canada

Lombard Street,
San Francisco, California, USA

Butchart Gardens, Victoria,
British Columbia, Canada